URBAN TRIBES

URBAN TRIBES

Are Friends the New Family?

ETHAN WATTERS

BLOOMSBURY

First published in Great Britain 2004

Copyright © 2003 by Ethan Watters

The moral right of the author has been asserted

Bloomsbury Publishing Plc, 38 Soho Square, London W1D 3HB

A CIP catalogue record for this book is available from the British Library

ISBN 0 7475 6587 2

10 9 8 7 6 5 4 3 2 1

All papers used by Bloomsbury Publishing are natural,
recyclable products made from wood grown in
well-managed forests. The manufacturing processes
conform to the environmental regulations of the
country of origin.

Typeset by Hewer Text Ltd, Edinburgh
Printed in Great Britain by Clays Ltd, St Ives plc

For Rebecca

CONTENTS

THE RELUCTANT TREND SPOTTER

What right do I have to speak for my generation?

A question like that can hit you pretty hard when you are staring into a hotel mirror at some ungodly hour of the morning, after a sleepless night, about to make your first appearance on *Good Morning America*. I know because this happened to me not long after I wrote a two-page magazine story coining the phrase "urban tribes." For reasons that were never made entirely clear, the producers thought I was a generational expert who could explain why the number of "never-marrieds" had more than doubled in a single generation. Who were these people who were delaying marriage, they wanted to know, and what were they doing with their lives? I had been flown to New York to summarize the lifestyles and life choices of 37 million youngish Americans.

At such an early hour, that hotel mirror seemed to reflect both me and the ideas that I was there to expound darkly. To say that I saw in that mirror everything I hated about our shoot-from-the-hip, craze-crazy American culture might be putting it too harshly. I definitely wondered what the hell I was doing, going on national television to talk about a demographic group I had yet to fully understand. I wasn't completely without ideas. I had noticed something in my life that I felt might go a long way toward explaining the lifestyle of those in Western countries who were delaying marriage into their late twenties, thirties, and forties. I had the notion that they were forming communities and influencing culture in a way that we had yet to fully appreciate. But it was only a glimpse; I had not had the time to take a close look.

In addition to this problem, I had a general reluctance to become part of the trendsetting industry. To grow up in the industrialized world in the later part of the twentieth century was to feel assaulted with trends. From the time my generation was old enough to have an allowance, wily marketers had been trying to get us on some band-wagon or another. Now that we were earning decent salaries, often with no children to support, we possessed, as a group, a disposable income that dwarfed the defense budget, and everyone with money to advertise was taking aim at us. It was a simple formula: Find an insecurity (weight, loneliness, body odor), exaggerate that worry to the point where we felt self-conscious, then offer up the "solution" (a diet, a self-help book, a matchmaking service, a deodorant).

Was I no different or better than these heartless marketers? Finding insecurities to prick among those who had delayed marriage was easy, because we had so many. We worried that our lives were not as meaningful as those lived in families. We worried also that we were more selfish and less community minded than our parents. Perhaps most pervasively, we worried that there was something wrong with us that kept us from finding love. In creating the idea of "urban tribes," was I just another soulless shill pandering to a demographic group that has known, since kindergarten, only the pursuit of self-gratification?

The request to appear on the show had felt something like a summons. I didn't know that producers from morning shows called and expected you to walk out of your life RIGHT NOW and fly to New York so they could wake you up at six A.M. the next day (three A.M. if you are, like I am, from the West Coast) and put you on national television. It didn't occur to me to say no. I was put up in a fancy hotel on Times Square that included a miniature Japanese rock garden (complete with a pencil-sized wooden rake to smooth the sand) that utterly failed to calm my nerves.

The fact that I didn't fully understand the ideas I had been invited to tell the nation about became sickeningly clear when I attempted to describe my concept of the urban tribe to myself in that hotel mirror. I knew my interviewer would ask me what an urban tribe was, but try as I might, I couldn't put the answer together. "An urban tribe comes from the time of life we spend while we're single when we don't have someone to marry because we're not . . . lonely . . . but . . . we . . . are . . ." I said as a nauseating panic rose in my chest. I stopped, took a deep breath and tried again. "Urban tribes come from our need for a time when we are not spending . . . many . . . years . . . being . . ." Another try: "Never-marrieds like myself need urban tribes because when we're single, they're the nature of communities that we don't have after we . . . college . . . ourselves . . ."

The words all sounded like they might be useful, but they were definitely not coming out in a coherent order. The problem was more than just sleeplessness mixed with stage fright. The tiny magazine article I had written had little to do with any national trend. I had seen something in my life: namely, that after nearly two decades of being single my group of friends in San Francisco seemed to form a coherent community. I had noticed that this personal community of mine had not only provided me consistent emotional support but had come to influence every choice I made in life, from how I comported my romances to the risks I took in my career. I guessed that others in my circumstances might be living in similar urban tribes, but in truth I had no idea whether people were living similar lifestyles in Detroit, L.A., or New York or for that matter Montreal, London, Paris, or Sydney.

If you've ever had the dream that you had to take a final exam after never attending class, you may have some small inkling of the nightmare I was living. I was about to be quizzed on national television on a topic I knew precious little about. Trying to calm myself, I made some hotel-room coffee and forced down a Luna bar. I left a voice mail for my girlfriend back in San Francisco telling her not to watch the show when she got up. Then I threw up the Luna bar and went down to the lobby to meet the network page who was to take me to the studio.

In the greenroom for *Good Morning America* I met Jim Karas, a handsome young personal trainer and the author of *Business Plan for Your Body*. He had the sort of face and personality that light up a room, and it was clear to me why he had become something of a regular on the show. Dressed in a stylish workout suit, Karas was scheduled to go on after me, accompanied by a young female client of his, to demonstrate exercises proven to firm up one's legs. This seemed odd to me at first, because the young woman's legs looked shapely and toned. This confusion was quickly cleared up when I figured out that "legs" actually means "ass" in the puritanical parlance of morning television. When Karas learned that I was a fellow author and that I had never before been on a morning talk show, he kindly tried to calm my nerves.

"Nobody remembers what you say on these shows. Just being here and looking good is the thing," he said with his winning smile. "Nobody wants you to fail. You'll see; it will be as easy as can be."

As the morning went on, I began to understand what he meant. Morning television shows rely on their guests to be relatively articulate and interesting, so the producers and staff are adept at convincing you in a short time that, even in your state of near-catatonic fear, everything is going to be fine. The staff you meet before you go on air are like horse whisperers, except they employ their soothing powers on nervous people. I soon met Fred, whose job it was, ostensibly, to run a microphone cord up my shirt and fasten a pager-sized transmitter to my belt. His real job, I suspected, was as a people whisper. His movements, demeanor, and facial expressions were so calm and reassuring that I became mildly hypnotized. When Fred asked me if I wanted a mint, I nearly cried with gratitude. It's not that I wanted a mint, but that little bit of kindness and normalcy seemed to shake me out of the nightmare scenarios of public humiliation playing over and over again in my brain. I had to restrain myself from giving Fred a hug.

As the large clock on the greenroom wall ticked steadily toward my 8:08 time slot, I met the woman who would appear with me. Gillian was a blond corporate lawyer from Philadelphia, selected unscientifically because she was a family friend of one of the *Good Morning America* producers. She was to represent those women who desired to find a husband but had inexplicably delayed getting married and

4

having a family. She was a good fit for the role. She was attractive, smart, and a fast and funny talker with confidence to spare. I assumed lots of nice, smart guys (who maybe lacked J. Crew looks or super-high-powered careers or some other impossible-to-meet criteria) had had their hearts crushed by Gillian. Given her charming smile and obvious confidence, I assumed that she hadn't gotten married because she had selfishly held out for Mr. Perfect.

"What do you think they are going to ask me?" she said as we were ushered toward the set.

"Well, I think they are going to ask you why you're not married," I said.

"Oh God," she said. "You really think so?"

When our time finally came, we were motioned to a seat on the set of what was supposed to look like a living room. Huge bugs in the guise of television cameras began sizing me up with their Cyclops-like eyes. Then, in the midst of the nightmare, I saw a calm and friendly face, an angel in the form of Diane Sawyer. Fred's power as a people whisperer was nothing in comparison with the hypnotic trance Diane Sawyer cast on me. People behind the cameras were saying something about commercials and then counting back from five. Out of the corner of my eye, Gillian asked me something. She said, "Quick, give me an answer, why aren't I married?"

"I can't help you," I said, never taking my eyes off Sawyer's dazzling smile. Everything was going to be okay, the smile said. Diane Sawyer was talking straight to one of the cameras; then she turned to me and asked me a question. While I remember only vaguely what the question was, I do recall that she phrased it in such a way as to make it impossible not to answer. Easy questions are sometimes described as softballs, meaning that they are hard not to hit out of the park. The question Diane Sawyer asked was much easier than that, as the answer was imbedded in the question. I merely had to take the question mark off the end of the sentence, rearrange a couple of words, and repeat it back to her. She had not pitched me a softball – she had held the ball in front of me, risking her tiny, delicate, perfectly manicured fingers, and, with her eyes, told me the moment I was to swing away.

Then it was over. I was back in the greenroom with a rising euphoria in my chest. I ran into Jim Karas, who was stretching in preparation for telling America how to firm up its ass.

"You looked great. I told you it would be easy," he said. "Every time I appear on this show, my book goes to number one on Amazon. All I have to do is show up at these shows and look good. People aren't buying the book because of what I've written."

What struck me about Karas's statement was its complete lack of cynicism. He wasn't against people reading his book, and I'm sure he made a sincere effort to fill his pages with useful information on diet and exercise. Karas was simply stating God's honest truth about the nonfiction book industry – especially the diet, self-help, and trend/lifestyle categories. I already knew that such books were sold to publishers based on short proposals that usually became the introductions. Those introductions are the only piece of the book that gets read, because it's the only part that is readable – the rest is endless variations on a single theme. Karas understood and was at ease with the fact that these books were packaged, promoted, and marketed to be bought but seldom read – certainly not cover to cover.

As kind and honest as Karas was being, he was killing my buzz. I suddenly wondered, there in the greenroom of *Good Morning America*, why we, as a culture, inflate writers into "experts." I guess it's nice to know that a culture that reads less and less still respects writers enough to give them some free airtime. But if the two writers in the greenroom of *Good Morning America* that day were any indication, this veneration had become something of a confidence game. One of us was at ease with the knowledge that people may not be reading his book, and the other – myself – was even more suspect. I had just offered my opinion to millions of sleepy-eyed Americans – good Lord, I had stepped into the role of *spokesperson for my generation* – with these dubious credentials: I had written a two-page magazine piece.

Feeling suddenly as if I were leaving the scene of a crime, I went back to my hotel to gather my things. On the hotel voice mail, I picked up a message from a friend and fellow writer in California. "Congratulations on your first of what will be many ax blows into the cultural consciousness of America," the message went. "I think the show probably got pretty good ratings. You were up against Katie Couric having her colon examined."

As I flew back west that night watching an hour-long sunset, my dread deepened. America needed another trend, another catchy coinage, like it needed another salty treat to stuff down its bloated snack hole. Urban tribes, the yet-to-be-marrieds, generation this that or the other – oh Lord, protect us from those who would pin us wriggling to the wall in five words or less.

Back home, I didn't turn my computer on for a couple of weeks. When I did, I found more than five hundred e-mails. Before I had gone to New York, a computer-savvy friend of mine had helped me set up a Web site describing my urban tribe and encouraging people to send me stories about their lives and the social structures they had created to sustain them during their time outside of families. With the help of my television appearance, word had gotten around, and I was besieged by folks who wanted to tell me how they were living during this time.

As I began reading, I was immediately impressed by the joyful and smart way people wrote about their lives. Their messages were a seamless mix of personal anecdotes, observations, cultural reportage, and life philosophy. In one e-mail, a correspondent might analyze her life using a fact she had learned in college about ape behavior, a personal story of a friendship, a plot line she had seen on television, and a lesson from her parents.

This sort of eclectic social commentary was familiar: It was exactly the way my friends and I talked about our lives. In trying to chart the landscape of our early adulthood, we drew no sharp distinction between highbrow and lowbrow knowledge. We stitched together our life philosophies from song lyrics, sacred texts, our college social

7

psychology classes, our parents, our bosses and coworkers, *The Simpsons,* snippets of wisdom forwarded to us in e-mails, and things we overheard on the bus. For us, the answer to the question How do you live a good life? was not something handed down from on high. We were making up answers – riffing them – as we went along.

Reading my e-mails, I quickly learned that there was nothing like an average urban tribe or an average postcollege/prefamily life. Most of these people seemed to have created community through friends in cities, but they were unwilling to let me simplify it. The size, composition, rules, and rituals of these groups varied dramatically. Many people described lives lived bouncing between two or more core groups. One group had formed around college friends, while another had formed in a workplace. Some groups had existed for a decade or more and had several dozen members, while others described tribes of three or four members that had been together less than a year. Some were all of one gender and race, while others were remarkably diverse. Some groups had strict rules that no intragroup sex was allowed, while others described what appeared to be ongoing bacchanalia.

The complexity and heterogeneous nature of these accounts was staggering. It appeared that the lives of young adults were varying in every imaginable way. It was no wonder that we had been so hard to pigeonhole as a generation. Even the commonalities that seemed to lump us together, such as the fact that we were getting married later, hid a more interesting truth that split us apart. Yes, on average we were getting married later, but we were also getting married over a much wider range of years. We were as likely to be trying to begin families at twenty-five as at thirty-five. The same wide variation could be seen in our careers. Some worked decades for a single company; some jumped around from job to job. Entrepreneurship and freelancing had become commonplace. Sex out of wedlock, while ubiquitous, ran the gamut of actual practices from monogamous relationships to musical beds. No one seemed up to the job of telling us how we should live.

We were facing the challenges of lives navigated without signposts and, not surprisingly, we had headed in many different directions. Unlike some, I certainly never expected sympathy for our excess of freedom. Life presents difficulties to every generation, and the challenges inherent in the choices my generation had were a fortunate burden to bear. In one way, we had been in training our whole lives for this challenge. Raised during a time of remarkable wealth, our potential has always felt unlimited. We could be anything we wanted, our parents had told us from birth, and we believed them almost too well. All paths were open. Women and men alike could delay marriage to pursue careers, or delay careers to travel, or delay travel to pursue education – or vice versa and the other way around.

As I corresponded and talked with more and more of the people who contacted me, I began to feel as if we were all on a grand adventure. Not long ago, the course of one's life would, in all likelihood, be an expression of one's class and group membership. How exciting that we had the freedom to shape our lives to be an expression of personal character.

Not that it was easy. Some, for example, chose to simply delay, period. With no map to navigate one's life, some of us have stood stock-still. In such a world of confused roles, time lines, and expectations, the simplest decisions could sometimes become problematic. This was the humor of *Seinfeld*: It was a comedy of manners in an era when the manners were all in flux. Forget figuring out how to chart a career and start a family; some of us, like the characters on *Seinfeld*, couldn't figure out how to go to the movies.

So what was the purpose of a trend book if we are all taking different paths? Let me not overstate my point here. Our spectrum of personal choices, while in some ways unparalleled, was not infinite and certainly was not random. Commonalities were there to be found, not the least of which was that we were all facing so many choices. As I began to read the e-mail and correspond with those who had contacted me, I discovered that nearly every one of them expressed some ambivalence about their wide-ranging options. They knew they were privileged to have these choices, but they also knew the stakes were high. These people were asking the big questions: How do I find meaning in my life? Should I have children? What is the most meaningful way to connect with other people? How should I balance my work life with my personal life (and is there even a distinction anymore)? Will I fall in love and marry?

This is not to say that we were completely alone with these questions. Even in times of change and flux, it is important to remember that shared social narratives influence our conceptions of our own lives and happiness. A life – even one's own – is too complicated a thing to hold in the mind, and this is why we need to identify with stories of others living in our time. It is only through the sharing of these cultural narratives that we can give coherence and meaning to our existence. This may sound like esoteric stuff, but the point is that important things in our own lives can go unseen or misunderstood if we lack the story template in our cultural vocabulary to describe them.

"We tell ourselves stories in order to live," wrote Joan Didion a generation ago. "We live entirely by the imposition of a narrative line upon disparate images, the shifting phantasmagoria which is our actual experience." This quote is out of context, for she was speaking here of a time following the sixties when she lost the ability to use stories to find meaning. Nevertheless, she continued to tell stories – ones that were dark and disjointed and lacked clear moral lessons. And in doing so she proved something remarkable about stories: Their value is not in their morals or in their ability to reduce life's complexity to simple sets of causation. Even if it reveals a world that is phantasmagoric in its complexity, the story still, almost magically, provides solace and meaning. To live without a story is to live without a sense of coherence and momentum. And there's another risk. Not to have a narrative of your own is to become susceptible to those imposed upon you by forces around you. I'm thinking about *Generation X*, *Less than Zero*, and all the other dismal portrayals of the post-baby-boom generation.

It seemed to me that we were living in something of a narrative vacuum. It was in hopes of helping fill this emptiness that hundreds of people were offering to tell me about their lives. They expressed a deep desire to know how their thoughts and their life choices were the same as or different from those of others in similar circumstances. That we were a generation with a tremendous diversity of life paths was itself a narrative that we needed to understand and begin to share. There was group solace in knowing that our group was so various – that there was in fact no simple socially accepted or expected course for a young adult to follow today.

You may have surmised by this point that this introduction is not going to summarize what I've learned about urban tribes and the marriage delay. I want to share with you not simply my conclusions but also the journey, and even some of the detours, I took to find them. If you need another reason to come along for the trip (as opposed to waiting for my next appearance on television where I will stumble to spit out the "talking points"), I'll give it to you. The pop-cultural debate about trends that occurs on television and radio feeds off bad news. This is because it's far easier to be pessimistic in short bursts than it is to be optimistic. One can easily point to the marriage delay, for example, and make the case that everything is going to hell. (After all, isn't the marital union civilization's basic unit – its carbon atom – of community?) But to understand why things might be changing for the better requires many more data points than one can possibly rattle off before the next commercial break. It requires that we not just look at national statistics and demographic trends but try to integrate them with the convoluted stories of people's actual lives.

A couple of months after my brief television appearance I was traveling through Philadelphia and had breakfast with Gillian. She turned out to be very little like the woman I had thought I met on the set of *Good Morning America*. The role she had been picked to play on television, Successful Woman Who Eschews Marriage and Family, didn't fit her at all.

In the months after we had first met she had quit her corporate-lawyer job and taken a $40,000 pay cut to work at a firm that specializes in employee discrimination. She was not Ms. Picky but admitted to deep insecurities about dating and her hopes of getting married in time to have a family. As we talked, I learned that she hadn't chosen to avoid marriage. As she described it, the currents of her life seemed to have drifted her away from the altar.

What I saw before me was a smart woman who was living a life driven by personal conviction and who, at the same time, felt bewildered and tossed around by cultural trends and forces she had no control over or even names for. I listened to her and I told her about my life. We compared our choices and thoughts. I had no easy answers for her and she had none for me, but together we began to tell the story of our time.

PART ONE

FREEDOM AND COMMUNITY

Chapter 1

CONFESSIONS OF A YET-TO-BE-MARRIED

"What ever happened to getting married?" I asked a carful of friends. This was half a dozen years ago while we were on our way to Burning Man. The U-Haul trailer we were pulling carried two dozen eight-foot lengths of two-by-fours, thirty bedsheets, a couple hundred yards of rope, thirty cases of beer, and all the other makings for our homegrown art project. Our plan was to string the sheets, à la Christo, along the desert, then offer other Burning Man attendees an ice-cold Sapporo beer for writing a properly constructed haiku on the sheets. Burning Man, a kind of wacky desert art festival, was a yearly event for my group of friends. Along with the makings for our interactive art installation, we had approximately twenty pounds of Gummy Bears, fifteen pounds of Twizzlers, food for five days, three hundred gallons of water, a variety of costumes, and one hundred green glow sticks so we could keep track of each other in the desert night. A total of twenty-five friends were headed from San Francisco across the Sierra toward our rendezvous in the Black Rock Desert that day. Significantly absent among them was Julia, my girlfriend at the time.

It was because of that absent girlfriend that the subject of marriage had been on my mind, the issue having recently and contentiously come up between the two of us. I knew that others in the car had been thinking about it as well. We were all in our late twenties or early-to-middle thirties, yet none had found brides or husbands. Although we were all older than our parents were when they had us, the idea of having children ourselves still seemed a far-off abstraction that came up only when someone asked whether we "wanted" children.

There was a growing sense among us that our postcollege/prefamily life was stretching into an awfully long time – five, ten, almost fifteen years for some – and that maybe we had missed a turn somewhere. Our parents, having suffered through introductory dinners with a half-dozen to a dozen prospective mates, were becoming concerned. They worried for us, or, if they were less generous or more eager for grandchildren, accused us of being "slackers," a word they had come to understand from listening to public radio.

Jen, a fast-thinking criminal defense lawyer who was often first out of the block with her notions, answered first.

"Women have their own careers and resources and they no longer need the institution of marriage to survive," she said. Jen had grown up in middle-income New Jersey but had managed to shake off most of the trappings of that life in her hipper, less-permed California incarnation. "It's simple economics. Most women still want to get married, but fewer women feel like they have to. Besides, we have those things to help open jars now."

"It's the breakdown of tradition in the city," said Adam, a documentary filmmaker and true child of left-wing Berkeley. "Our families can't force us to do anything anymore, and the church has even less power. We put ourselves first now. We can't get married because we're tragically selfish."

"It's simpler than that. We're not getting married because it's no longer required before having sex," offered Josh, a tall, handsome underachiever who was always pragmatic when it came to sexual issues and opportunities. "You know, if the milk is free, who's going to sell the cow?"

"You mean 'buy the cow' – 'no one wants to *buy* the cow.' " Jen said, hitting Josh on the back of the head. "It's a wonder you get any milk at all."

"I think our generation grew up with too much marital carnage," Alice offered tentatively. A graduate student in her late thirties, she was new to our group and was still getting the hang of how we talked

16

about the world. "We spent our adolescence ducking and covering as families up and down the block went off like bombs. We get post-traumatic-stress symptoms just going home for Thanksgiving, like revisiting a combat zone."

I paused, as they waited for my theory. I could see that all their ideas had merit. But even though it was true that the idea of marriage had lost some of its traditional importance and had been grievously damaged by the ice-storm divorces of the seventies, we all claimed that we still desired it. We often talked of marriage as if it were the finish line of this leg of life's race. There seemed to be something more going on with our delay, something getting in our way.

"I've been thinking that, for me, the problem is you guys," I said, pausing to let that sink in. "I mean, how would I get the momentum up to get married when I'm always hanging around with my friends? I spend more time *talking* about my love life with you all than I do *having* one."

"And I thought Julia wasn't coming on this trip," Josh said in a stage whisper to Jen. "But look, he's channeling his girlfriend for us."

"You know what my dad was doing when he was my age?" I continued, a little riled by Josh's comment. "He had a steady job, he was married to my mom, and they were having me. I can also tell you what he *wasn't* doing: He wasn't driving to the desert with two dozen of his friends to build a haiku-for-beer camp."

"Worse than channeling," Jen said with mock concern. "I think Julia's possessed his body. Ethan, are you in there? Quick, someone call a priest."

As annoying as they were, my friends were right. I *was* speaking for Julia, who had recently, in a series of intense arguments, all but convinced me that my life was stuck. It had started because the weekend of Burning Man had conflicted with her best friend's wedding in her hometown of Athens, Georgia. I had ill-advisedly suggested that my group's yearly pilgrimage to Burning Man was equally important to me as the wedding of her friend was to her. Not only would Julia not concede this point, she found it jaw-droppingly bizarre that I would even make such a comparison.

17

The fights became intense because the wedding–versus–Burning Man debate was emblematic of Julia's belief that my friends were stunting my growth – delaying my graduation to a more adult existence. She would list the details of my life as if that conclusion were obvious: In my early thirties, I was a freelance writer making a hand-to-mouth living. I shared a large flat with a Zen monk, a musician, a filmmaker, and three other people. I insisted on being at the Rite Spot restaurant every Tuesday night, when my group of friends would meet for dinner. I attended so religiously that I would schedule trips not to miss these Tuesday gathering. Julia had one or two close friends, but she couldn't see the point in carrying on, as I did, with a group of two dozen. "Your life is Seinfeldian," she told me, "except with all Georges. You know what that show is about? Nothing."

Was my life about nothing? I had to admit that Julia made a convincing case, and I was vulnerable to the criticism. My life often felt like a montage of happy, often slapstick, scenes, but I couldn't make the case that it had much of a plot. There I was holding the boom microphone on the set of a friend's independent film. Cut to a scene of my group of friends lounging in the moonlight on the roof of a houseboat listening to Noah play the guitar. Cut to the shared dinners or the roommate meetings or the writing groups . . . It didn't matter how you strung these scenes together, they didn't add up to any narrative I knew.

I wasn't joking about the idea that my friends were the problem. It would be hard, after all, to realize that your life was off track if everybody in your frame of reference was similarly derailed. Like myself, my friends were all leading busy and upbeat postcollege/prefamily lives. They lived alone or with roommates and worked along in their careers. In their love lives, they suffered through two-year cycles that went from singleness to crush to relationship to heartbreak and back to singleness. We absolved ourselves from these failures by believing that we just hadn't met the right person. Hope springs eternal with romantic desire, and that "right person" excuse was easy for us to accept as individuals. But as we stepped back and saw that everyone around us was delaying marriage, that excuse was harder to swallow. Were there no "right people" left? An unsettling *Twilight Zone*–ish feeling was creeping in as we were exceeding the age our parents were when we first knew them.

I had never planned to live my twenties and early thirties in this manner. After college, my girlfriend and I moved to a low-rent neighborhood of San Francisco assuming that we were in a brief transition period between college and marriage. We lived together for one year and then another. We waited as if the decision to get married would decide itself on its own. It didn't, and she eventually left me to move on to graduate school. Being young and full of hope at the time, I assumed the problem was with the timing and discontents of that particular relationship and not with me. I began searching the city for my true love, assuming that this wouldn't take too long.

I didn't know it back then, but I was a harbinger of a massive trend. Like most modern singles, I wasn't just looking for a suitable spouse; I was soul-mate searching. Although I disliked the phrase's New Age connotations, I counted myself among the 94 percent of my fellow never-marrieds who, when asked in a Gallup poll, agreed that when you marry, you want your spouse to be your soul mate first and foremost. Along with my friends, I discovered that searching for a soul mate wasn't so easy. Although I dated smart and charming women, the soul-mate standard I tried to apply was so elusive in my own mind that any disgruntlement could become a reason for the big what-are-we-doing? talk. I wasn't looking for that certain something, a friend once cruelly observed, I was looking for that certain *everything*.

We were a curious new breed, those of us treading water in the cities – outside of our families of origin and seemingly unwilling to begin families for ourselves. We were interested in (often devoted to) our careers and avocations, but we stayed strangely off the social map in other ways. Devotion to blood ties didn't seem to interest us enough to stay in our hometowns, and the idea of finding community among our neighbors was a quaint anachronism. While we worried about the "breakdown of community" and bemoaned the current level of selfishness in the country, we didn't seem to be taking much action. Although we were part of the fastest-growing demographic group in America, our Census Bureau designation, the "never-marrieds," implied a type of stasis – we were a population defined by what we *weren't* doing.

It seemed that for years I had been on the hunt for a story line for my life, but I had come up empty. I had read the books and had seen the movies that purported to portray my demographic of young single urban dweller: *Slacker*, *Clerks*, *Generation X*, all the way back to *Less Than Zero* and *Bright Lights, Big City*. Sometimes these storytellers even backed up their sad narratives with statistics of their own. In *Generation X*, Douglas Coupland clearly meant to frighten us when (on the same page that told us a "finely ground" pound of plutonium can kill forty-two billion people) he reported a remarkable rise of the number of never-marrieds among twentysomethings. Coupland gave no commentary on this fact, because the meaning was clear: As a generation we were in grave trouble.

If we spent five to fifteen years not devoted to a spouse or children – what *did* we care about? The assumption was that we cared only about ourselves.

I carried a burden of responsibility for this selfish disaffection having become the story of our time. As one employed among the ranks of pop-culture makers – those who write movies, books, magazine articles, and television shows – I knew that our tone of voice was *expected* to be cynical and disconnected. When I profiled rock stars, I presented their nihilism without irony. I wrote personal essays about how emasculating it was to be renting at thirty with little hope of ever buying a house in San Francisco. Many of the writers I shared an office with were turning out the same dark stories. It was easy to portray our demographic as prone to breakups and bowling alone, and as a pose it had its advantages. We could all act like the star in our own gritty urban drama, pretending that every turn in our lives was portentous. It made for good copy. Anyway, better to have a depressing story to live by than face the anxiety of having none at all.

But I already knew there was something wrong with that story. First of all, we weren't nearly as depressed as we sometimes made ourselves sound. Those who shared my demographic (single, young adult, professional, urban dweller) were only seldom chronically sad. I did meet some people who *dressed* as slackers, but I never came across those who had lowered their hopes to the point where they aspired only to get stoned and wallow in pop-culture trivia. While we were often willing to strike the pose of the urban disaffected (we were practically required to if we were artists, musicians, or writers), that did not seem to represent the truth of our hearts.

But even if I was happy most of the time, what did it add up to? That's what Julia (and, secretly, my parents) wanted to know. Happiness comes in all guises, and I didn't want to defend a type of happiness that was shallow or transient. I couldn't convince her (or myself for that matter) that my life added up to much of anything. She had determined that single life in the city was a phase to be concluded as quickly as possible. She wanted to be getting married or at least be on track for begetting children. If that wasn't going to happen, she intended to move back to Athens to be near her parents and brother. The bonds of family were the ties that she understood and longed for; everything else seemed temporary and immature.

The fact that I didn't have ready answers to Julia's challenges was causing me anxiety. In short, I began to believe that Julia was right – that for the last ten years I had simply delayed becoming an adult. Which is why I would suggest to a carload of my friends, on the way to our favorite weekend of the year, that they were a millstone around my neck.

A Dreamscape of Community

It was late in the afternoon, with the sunlight slanting across that lunar landscape, when we finally turned off onto the four-hundred-square-mile alkaline mudflat that is the Black Rock Desert. This is the first thrill of Burning Man, driving the five miles across the featureless baked dirt, watching the festival grow in size as you approach. Finding the campsite that Rob had staked out the day before, we unloaded the gear. After that initial work, Jim started to fix an elaborate paella dinner. I wandered off to take my first look at that year's event.

I went from camp to camp with a Costco-sized plastic barrel of Twizzlers. This was the ethos of the place – bring something to share and make friends. In the camp next to us, I met a six-pack of beefy guys who all worked as bouncers in clubs around Seattle. They gave me a Red Bull as thanks for the licorice and invited me back later that night to hear their punk band, Meat Locker. Next to them was a group of twenty-somethings who knew each other from working in the high-tech industry in L.A. They were in the midst of setting up monster speakers and constructing a large geodesic dome made of PVC piping in preparation for a three-day dance party. A little further on was a group of ten friends who had driven all the way from Atlanta to build an eighteen-hole miniature golf course there in the Nevada badlands. To complete their project they had hauled with them nearly a half-acre of AstroTurf.

And on and on it went, camp after camp. There were more than twenty thousand people gathering there in the desert, almost all of them in small camps of friends engaged in some quixotic creative project. I had noticed that whenever Burning Man was covered in magazines or on television, it was portrayed as something of a freak show, where urban primitives came to get naked, cover themselves with mud, and set things on fire. To be sure, there was a sort of postapocalyptic carnival atmosphere there, but that wasn't the truth of the thing. Burning Man was the art-festival equivalent of moshing, a dance that, because people run into each other full force, appears to be the very expression of antisocial behavior. But those in the mosh pit (especially those who have fallen down and felt a half-dozen hands instantly lift them back onto their feet) know the secret: There are elaborate rules to moshing and an etiquette, to boot. Burning Man and moshing are not expressions of antisocial behavior but of a heartfelt desire for connection and community in the cool *guise* of rebellion – the best of both worlds.

After the licorice whips were all gone, I wandered away from the encampments across the open playa toward The Man. A four-story wooden effigy, The Man is physically and conceptually the central point of the event. He burns (or, more precisely, he explodes and then burns) on Saturday night. I climbed up a small mountain of haystacks at the base of the figure and watched below where two dozen Germans covered in Mazola oil were playing a slippery game of Twister. I wondered, sitting there, whether this would be my last trip to Burning Man. Probably Julia was right, I thought; I was getting too old for this. Perhaps it was time to move on and become a real adult.

The sun had just hit the horizon when I first caught a glimpse of a large vehicle moving across the desert. The thing was maybe a mile off, but I could see that a massive mainsail of the type you might find on a fifty- or sixty-foot yacht powered it. As it got closer I saw that it rolled on three truck tires spread fifteen yards apart on a huge triangular metal frame. There were fifteen people on this land ship, cruising along at a sprinter's clip. There was a young man at the wheel and a woman, whom I surmised to be the captain, standing next to him shouting commands. Watching this behemoth approach, I tried to imagine the teamwork necessary to build that vehicle, the hours of cooperation it took to create this impressive machine and haul it to this forbidding landscape. The Germans untangled themselves from their game to hoot and applaud as we watched the ship tack around The Man and head downwind, toward the sunset. What a sight: a team of friends sailing across the desert.

Walking back, I spotted my own camp from a few hundred yards off because someone had started the generator and strung up Christmas lights around our compound. I could see a few of my friends putting up their tents, but most were gathered around a small fire where Jim was cooking his paella and Rob was strumming his guitar. There were Rae and Larry, who had been my roommates for the last four years, and Po and Noah, who had been my writing partners and officemates for longer. There was Jake, who was always up for taking an expedition out of town to explore a river or a mountain, and Christine and Jen, who counseled me, usually with disastrous consequences, on my love life. It looked like home, that little encampment in the dust – home because these particular people were there waiting for me.

And then I could see the scene in a different way – as an anthropologist might who was studying a group of great apes. It was almost dark now and I stopped twenty yards away, outside the glow of the Christmas lights. Certainly, each of these people had a relationship with me, but they all had distinct relationships with each other. There was a web of love affairs, friendships, rivalries, work partnerships, and shared homes. Connect any two of those twenty-five people and you would find a history of activities and hundreds of hours of conversation that held shared secrets, gossip, and all manner of insight about the world. Those relationships created an intricate web of lives that added up to more than the sum of the friendships. What I saw there in the late Nevada twilight was not a loose group of friends but a single entity of which I was a critical part. There it was, gathered around a campfire in the desert: an Urban Tribe.

And then that notion radiated out across that makeshift city. The boys from Meat Locker, the high-tech technoheads from L.A., the golfers from Atlanta, the slippery Germans, and, most of all, the friends on that land ship – I was surrounded by tribes like mine, all of them made up of groups of friends struggling to do something creative and support each other as they lived life between the families they grew up in and the families they might someday start for themselves. Maybe I had not been delaying my real life, as Julia insisted, but had been living it fully – sailing through my twenties and early thirties – as a member of a functional urban tribe. Maybe what I needed to do was not to push past this period but to embrace it and figure it out.

When I reached camp, Rob handed me a plate steaming with shrimp and salmon on a bed of flavored rice. Jen poured me a glass of red wine.

"Where have you been?" she asked. "We were wondering about you."

"I saw the most amazing thing out on the playa," I began.

24

Freedom and What We Did with It

That glimpse of my urban tribe out on the Black Rock Desert began the process of reassessing the time my friends and I were spending outside of families. That reassessment proved more difficult than I could have imagined at the time. Sadly, little of what I would come to understand about the tribe years would come to me in such revelatory flashes. What it meant to live for a decade or more outside of a traditional family proved hard to gauge. The changes affected by that sort of lifestyle over such an expanse of time were hard to discern in the bathroom mirror on a given morning.

At first the answers came by following little hints that appeared from time to time in my day-to-day life. One morning, for example, my roommate Larry was in our living room and declared, "Okay, it's settled, then: We'll transfer the home brew into bottles tomorrow morning, then we'll pick up the vacuum-cleaner motors for the hovercraft after we drop Rae off at therapy."

Larry said this some time after that trip to Burning Man. These are his exact words. I know because I began to repeat them like a mantra, having had the immediate sense that they revealed something true about my life, although at first I didn't fully understand what that was. Initially, I thought it added weight to Julia's conclusion that my life had become absurd. That these activities would be our primary goals for that next day – brewing beer, getting a friend to therapy, and building a homemade hovercraft – did seem ridiculous. It took me a while to see that there was more to it.

Let me provide some context about the scene in which that statement was made. It was a sunny mid-morning in the living room of my house in the Mission District of San Francisco. Rae was lying on the foldaway bed in the living room, where she had been sleeping since her ankle, which she had broken badly during the bike portion of a triathlon, made it too difficult to get upstairs to her bedroom in the attic. Our friend Thia was there, too; she didn't live with us but was between jobs and could be found at our house often, usually cooking in the kitchen. I was sitting on the couch, although I should have been writing.

Larry, who had recently moved back to the city after a few years living as a Zen monk on top of a mountain in Southern California, was in the midst of reintegrating into the nonmeditative world. He'd been filling his days taking odd construction jobs, working for a short time at an organic-vegetable delivery service, brewing beer, writing some songs, and generally trying to keep a step or two ahead of the existential dread that was his constant pursuer and/or companion. A month earlier, he had stumbled across an ad in a recent *Boys' Life* magazine that had captivated him twenty-five years before, when he was a skinny ten-year-old Catholic boy living with his large family in upstate New York. The ad sold instructions for how to build a one-man personal hovercraft. Larry sent away for the plans, and he took to building the thing in our basement while simultaneously writing a magazine story about the experience. Larry's intention to drive Rae to therapy with my car was part of a deal the two had made by which Larry would cook and care for Rae during the months when she couldn't put pressure on her ankle. The beer-brewing project (the beer was called Wath, for "While away the hours") was conceived as a means of giving them an entertaining project they could do together while they were homebound.

Although I remember many things about the day Larry said this, I do not remember exactly when it happened. It was after that trip to Burning Man, but that could mean two years ago or six. This vagueness has partly to do with seasons in San Francisco, which can pass from one to another without so much as a fifteen-degree fluctuation in the temperature, but probably has more to do with the fog of time that descended on me during those years. While I could remember the rough chronology of my work life, my social life was often so fluid and intent on the present moment (or the very next weekend) that in memory it became a disjointed, cutting-room-floor movie. My poor memory for when things happened was, I think, exaggerated by my personal disinclination/inability to plan into the future. Making the two-week cutoff to buy low-fare plane tickets seemed ridiculously farsighted.

As I thought about it, Larry's statement and the scene in our house at the moment that he said it revealed, in their ridiculousness, the truly embarrassing amount of freedom my friends and I were saddled with. Having delayed marriage into our late twenties and thirties, we lived with a remarkable amount of personal autonomy to make up our lives as we went along. This did not feel like some sort of multiple-choice freedom, but rather the type of freedom that could descend on us like a cyclone – erasing landmarks and spinning us around until we were dizzy with the complexity and sheer number of options that swirled around us. We didn't talk about it much, because freedom is a hard thing to identify in one's own life. Given that freedom is, for the most part, an absence of restraints, we rarely stopped to count the things we were not bound by. I decided that was exactly what I needed to do.

To begin with, I knew we were not tied down by family. I've already mentioned this, but it deserves emphasis. No generation before had delayed the starting of a family with the tenacity we had. Not only did most of us not have kids, but in certain hipster areas of major cities you could literally go days without *seeing* a child. Of course we had families in the form of parents and brothers and sisters. They were largely self-reliant, however, and only required our presence at major holidays and our voices over the phone every week or two. Our parents were living longer and more healthily. Even when they confronted illness, distance was often a wall to responsibility. Predictably, those of us who delayed marriage the longest were those who moved away to college and then to large metropolitan areas that promised interesting and consuming careers. We might have felt emotional accountability to our families back home (or wherever it was that our sisters and brothers landed), but it was seldom a drain on our time.

As for our parents' attempting to constrain or guide us from afar, mostly they didn't even try. By the time we hit twenty-five and had been living outside the house for six or seven years, either parents had abdicated their role of advice givers or we had stopped picking up the phone on Sunday mornings. Avoiding their calls was seldom necessary. Even when we were in high school and college, very few parents I knew seemed to be much interested in giving stern advice. While they encouraged us in our education, they did not, as a general rule, threaten disinheritance or any meaningful or lasting sanctions if we moved in with our girlfriends or boyfriends, bought a motorcycle, or quit our jobs to follow the lure of a deep certainly that we needed to become a Zen monk or a dot-com entrepreneur.

This reticence was true for virtually all traditional advice givers, from priests, to teachers, to bosses, to mentors. I can imagine a couple of reasons for their timidity. First, there was the mutual understanding between us and these erstwhile role models that their generation had no high horse to ride in on. We all understood, for instance, that it was their generation that had pioneered the record-setting divorce rates and that they were no strangers to the siren song of drugs, adultery, and other forms of self-destructive behavior. Every one of us had, during our adolescence, known an adult who was more confused and in need of guidance than we were at the time. The general social upheaval of the sixties and seventies left them with no solid front from which to attack with advice.

Only conservative politicians continued to give lifestyle advice as if it were still in style. It was pretty easy to read this for what it was: political posturing. George W. Bush's advice that we abstain from sex before marriage was an excellent example. Given that many of us were delaying marriage until we were thirty or thirty-five, his just-say-no-to-sex rhetoric read like a blatant pandering to the Christian Right or willful ignorance of social trends or both. Regardless of whether we voted for these conservative politicians, the idea that we would let their advice influence our personal choices was laughable.

Our freedom from strict life advice had a corollary: We were freer of the consequences of our actions than other generations. Our elders couldn't punish us for ignoring advice that had never been given in the first place. Of course, we weren't free from all consequences, contracting AIDS and being hit by a bus among them. (But for those who did not share intravenous drugs or practice unsafe sex, these two possibilities seemed equally easy to avoid. You were simply and routinely cautious every time you crossed the street or a bedroom threshold.) But in general there seemed plenty of forgiveness for mistakes – plenty of time to make everything right. We could date the wrong person for years, start on one career, quit, go back to school and try another. We had the sense that it could all be undone. We had moved to the city once to create a new adult self. If we wanted, we could move across town or across the country and do it again.

It was also clear that we had remarkable and historic freedom in how we pursued our romantic relationships. Although it would take me the next couple of years to understand what was happening in our love lives and figure out why we were delaying marriage, it was obvious that there was considerable flexibility in how we chose to mate. There was a multiplicity of socially acceptable options, from serial dating to serial monogamy to long-term relationships and marriage. There was some "hooking up," but no "free love" as such – a fact that no one seemed to bemoan. We could live together without shame. Or we could keep separate apartments from our significant others and go "home" to whichever place was close at the end of the day. Most of us in fact switched among these different paths over the years we stayed single. A serial dater might become a serial monogamist, with a long period of abstinence (chosen or not) in between.

Additionally, we were free from general social strife and the lockstep thinking of some national movement or other. We had no sense of a shared mission, no notion that we were a generation chosen for some higher purpose – whether to save the world from tyranny or to usher it into a new era of peace, love, and understanding. In college, we may have protested our university's investments in companies with holdings in South Africa, but as we went back to our dorm rooms at the end of our day, we all knew how estranged we were from the human destruction of apartheid. These protests were in the style of youthful anger, but they had little of its reckless intensity or frantic courage.

The fact that we picked such a distant and somewhat arbitrary cause to protest (no doubt our universities had investments in companies that had holdings in similarly repressive regimes) was telling. On the home front, we could not agree on a compelling cause to collectively champion.

It seemed also that we were freer than generations before us from ego-dampening hierarchies. I had never walked into a job where I felt it necessary to hold my tongue or give concerted respect or reverence to those older or higher up the food chain. Of course, I sometimes did give such respect, but it seemed voluntary on my part. There were few situations in which I was required to kowtow. This was perhaps a holdover from our college experiences, where the most sought-after teacher-student relationships were portrayed as partnerships in which, during rap sessions on this subject or another, teachers and students would "learn from each other." This led us to the belief that we could walk into any situation and assume that our opinions were probably as valuable as, if not more so than, the opinions of anyone else in the room.

What else were we free from? Here's a big one: We had the freedom of time. Spend five or ten years living among your friends, without the responsibility to care for a child or provide financial support for your spouse, and you'll discover that you have a lot of time to fill. Adding to this surplus of time, employers often gave twenty- and thirtysome-things "sabbaticals" that went up to half a year at a pop. We took long breaks in between jobs in the style and length of the summer vacations we had when we were in school. Of course it didn't *feel* as if we had a lot of time. We thought we were busy bees. But when we looked at the bags under the eyes of our older siblings who were managing babies and jobs while riding the emotional tides of their marriages as best they could, we knew the truth. (I once mentioned an article I read in the newspaper to my sister-in-law and she nearly wept, reminiscing about the days before motherhood when she too had time to read the paper.) We had plenty of time for our obsessions, time to flip through *Boys' Life* magazine and consider an investment of eighty hours to build that hovercraft that had floated in our boyhood imagination a quarter-century ago.

Women were freer to work in whatever field they chose. I knew it was not kosher to say that the battle for workplace equality had been won (there were income disparities that suggested otherwise), but from my personal perspective it might as well have been. During my time in the workforce, I had mostly women bosses. In general, women my age seemed to be smarter, better educated, and more capable and career oriented than I and most of the men I knew. I dated doctors, lawyers, editors, and ad executives, almost all of whom made more money than I did and drove nicer cars. Although I sometimes read in women's magazines that this was supposed to bother me, I don't remember being concerned. There was a riddle popular in the 1970s about the surgeon who says "I can't operate on this boy; he's my son!" after the boy has been injured in a car crash that killed his father. The riddle didn't befuddle my generation for an instant. We got the answer right away: The surgeon was the boy's mother.

During the boom years of the nineties we were largely free from money worries. My friends mostly had college educations and employers of all stripes were desperate for smart, warm bodies to fill their ergonomically correct chairs. In cities from Seattle to Austin, money was flowing steadily down the old light-industry corridors and into the hipper neighborhoods where many of us lived. In San Francisco, you could see the money coming down South of Market as warehouses and long-closed manufacturing plants were renovated into offices, restaurants, and lofts. You had to duck and cover to stay out of the way a decent paycheck.

Even when the economy turned and jobs and easy freelance gigs started to dry up, we didn't panic. For some of us money remained plentiful and for some of us money was scarce, but for the most part it didn't seem to be much of a factor in terms of influencing our life choices. In the long run, most of us knew we had an ace in the hole. Many of us were in line to be the beneficiaries of the largest transfer of wealth that had ever taken place from one generation to the next.

Something close to $10 trillion (roughly the size of the yearly gross domestic product of the United States) was in the process of being passed down to baby boomers and Generation Xers. Even if we hadn't yet benefited from our parents' savings and investments, or the increased value of the property they bought decades ago, we knew the wealth was there and someday headed our way. We didn't talk about this inevitable inheritance, given the terrible price we would pay for it, but I suspected that when we thought about our financial futures, we calculated in the fact that there was a windfall (sometimes a substantial one) coming to us some time before our own retirement. Why worry about saving for retirement when your parents have done that for you?

The plentiful work, combined with our future inheritances, allowed us to avoid making decisions based on money. At one extreme we could choose to be, like Larry, voluntarily poor. Talented with words and a dedicated worker, Larry could have been successful in any number of fields. Yet he chose to become a Zen monk (a notoriously poorly paid career) and after that a fifteen-dollar-an-hour handyman for friends who needed a room painted or cabinet built.

Although I knew only a few people who chose voluntary poverty, I knew equally few who pursued money single-mindedly and fewer still who made social judgments about the character of people based on their income or assets. In my group of friends there was an enormous range of wealth, from Larry, who was all but penniless, to a few friends who had ridden the e-business wave. (I knew several young millionaires and had met no fewer than *three* twentysomething billionaires.) There was little shame or social stigma attached to any financial status.

Having little reverence for money meant that we were free to spend whatever we had however we pleased. We had the temerity to zero out our bank accounts each month if we decided that we just had to buy that already antique Apple Newton (still in the box!) or that American Airlines baggage handler's jacket on eBay. If you saw a lot of us in television commercials, honking outside a friend's loft to show off our new Jettas, it's no wonder. As far as marketers and advertisers were concerned, we were the ripest peaches on the tree. A generation ago advertisers had a preference for the wealthy, but as they grew more sophisticated, they discovered that wealth – or, more precisely, disposable wealth – was relative to one's situation. In terms of her purchases, a twenty-five-year-old public relations person who made $40,000 could -- in certain situations – act as rich as an older married mother of two who earned $100,000. Subtract the house payments, the saving for college, the property taxes, the kids' school tuition, and the like, and marketers discovered that the twenty-five-year-old had as much, and sometimes more, money to throw around when she wandered into Tower Records on a Sunday afternoon. As significantly, the twenty-five-year-old had the *time* to do that sort of wandering.

So while some of us were voluntarily poor, most of us were situationally rich. Even the lower-income single person had one or two avocations or interests on which he or she spent money as if it were no object. The twenty-three-year-old assistant editor who made a measly $28,000 might eat macaroni and cheese every third night but spend money like a princess when she walked into the snowboarding shop or pay top dollar for an airline ticket to go to the New Orleans Jazz Festival. Within our various quirky avocations and interests we would tolerate only the best. We were "selectively affluent," as Joseph Turow explained in his book *Breaking Up America*, meaning that we sometimes spent like the rich even though we weren't.

Consequently, we were courted by everyone with something to sell – which led some of our college professors to suggest that, as a generation, we weren't free at all. Perhaps, they suggested, we were slaves in a capitalist system that manipulated our desires to keep us on a treadmill of purchases, vainly chasing after happiness through the stuff we bought. Is that what our freedom amounted to: freedom to spend?

Perhaps that was true for some. My own relationship with the market system felt more complex and far less nefarious. With the advent of marketing as a social science, the tables seemed to have turned on who was controlling whom. Outside of the kids' market-place, advertisers appeared to have lost the faith that they could manipulate us into wanting something and instead focused their considerable energy on trying to predict what we would want next. So, when Ikea played my favorite little-known alt-country band over its store stereo system one day, it felt less as if I were being perfectly manipulated and more as if some committee of sharp-eyed trend spotters was spending a lot of time and energy trying hard to please me. That our desires were being sated almost before we felt them gave us the sense that we were somehow directing commerce, not the reverse.

Marketing bull's-eyes like the one I experienced in Ikea that day were remarkably common. For a long time I frequented a perfect little café in San Francisco called Circadia. They did everything right: friendly table service, even for a cup of coffee; Internet access; live music three nights a week; a comfortable menagerie of chairs. The place felt hip and homegrown yet well run. Then I discovered it was a disguised Starbucks – a prototype where they studied new methods for future franchises. They had taken aim at my idea of the perfect coffeehouse and nailed it in every detail. After some initial anger that I had been seduced by Starbucks, I realized that I had to give them credit, and started to frequent the café again.

Should I have found it disturbing that there were hordes of de-viously smart people, ensconced in offices, studying people just like me to figure out not only what I would want to purchase but also what music I wanted to hear while shopping? I guess maybe I should have been disconcerted, but honestly I wasn't. I had to hand it to them when they did it well. It was no easy task to follow my directionless swim through cultural currents or to track my horribly vague, often contra-dictory, usually ironic, and always shifting "sense of style." It was nice of them to spend all that energy studying what, I, Ethan Watters, would want next.

Because, as I've already suggested, freedom is an absence of restraints, we didn't necessarily realize or talk about just how free we were. Only rarely, when we lifted our heads from our lives and looked around at the larger social landscape, did we see that our lives were different. This sometimes happened when we went back to our smaller hometowns for high school reunions or visited our siblings' families. Mostly, however, it didn't occur to us that we were different, because we were surrounded by people like ourselves, who similarly had the freedom to treat their lives as if they were one big fun hobby.

There was not even an order in which we were expected to take on life's challenges. "The predictable sequence of education, stable employment, marriage and parenthood, that marked earlier cohorts of young adults gave way to an increasing diversity of life paths," wrote Paul R. Amato and Alan C. Booth in their book, *A Generation at Risk*. "For these young adults the options were broader – and the outcomes less certain – than those available to their parents."

I can hear some baby boomers loudly objecting at this point. "What about the sixties? Weren't those the times of true generational freedom, when the old status quo was broken and brave new lifestyles explored? Wasn't that when times were really a-changin'?" No doubt, the sixties were a time of change. But for the individual they were still a time of clear social roles and expectations, even if one of those expectations was to subvert the expectations of the previous generation by rolling naked in the muddy fields at Woodstock. I got this notion from reading Wendy Kaminer, who observed, "Anyone who lived through [the sixties] knows that it was a much more self-righteous than relativistic period . . . Even the notorious 'permissiveness' of the '60s reflected prevailing dogmas . . . The counterculture didn't eschew moral codes: instead it rejected particular notions of moral behavior associated with the 1950s and replaced them with alternative moralities." Which is probably why, when the lifestyle of baby boomers swung, en masse, toward yuppiedom, no one was really surprised.

But if we were truly living in a time of unparalleled personal choice, where was all the fanfare? As I thought about it, it made sense that this sort of freedom might have been taking place quietly. As Kaminer implies, when individual freedom becomes the rally cry of the mob, you know you are witnessing something else entirely. (Everybody, chant together: "We are all different!") The test of freedom would be action, not ideology. Anyone can claim to be free of social constraints, but the truest gauge of that freedom is the degree to which individuals in a population choose different paths. Was it possible that my generation was living and struggling with the personal freedoms that baby boomers forged as a generation but individually only playacted?

Friends: The Problem or the Answer

Were we doing anything worthwhile with all this freedom? To be perfectly honest, I wasn't exactly sure. I knew how it looked, however. If you took a glance at our lives, we were often hard to like. If you were to read the text of the scenes played out by my group of friends, they would often sound comically selfish and self-absorbed. Indeed, we thought of ourselves this way. In a survey of men and women between the ages of twenty-five and thirty-five, over half described themselves as either "slackers" or "apathetic." In addition, they overwhelmingly believed their demographic group to be selfish, with fully 77 percent reporting that people of their generation were out for themselves.

If you looked only at many of the activities we engaged in, you might quickly agree. We had all this good fortune and freedom and what were we doing with it? Building personal hovercrafts and brewing homemade beer? Larry's projects were not at all unusual, at least not among my friends in San Francisco. Our lives often seemed quite literally composed of one such quixotic endeavor after the next. We joyfully trucked art projects to the desert for the Burning Man festival and then burned them in a ritual fire. We threw hootenannies for the neighborhood and started ironic country bands. We explored the urban wilderness of the abandoned Hunters Point shipyards. One friend, Todd, had transformed his apartment into a mini-museum for 1950s airline memorabilia, while another, Brad, had a collection of outdated technology. Ben created art using underpasses as his canvas.

We wrote songs and short stories about each other's love lives. We planned elaborate costumed Halloween trips to Vegas. Our pop-culture interests in *The Simpsons* or electronica music or in hacker culture bordered on the obsessive.

We had no authority figure to be the voice of reason with such interests, and we were each reluctant to take on such a role for our friends. It was so much easier to encourage their interests and dreams. When you went to your friends and said, "I think I'm going to build a recording studio in my spare room and become a record producer," they could be counted on to say something along the lines of "What a fantastic idea. Can I help?" "Yes, of course you should go trek the Himalayas," we would advise another friend, "you've been complaining about your job for months." "Re-create our senior prom? Sounds like a great idea! I know a hall we can rent." "You're becoming a whitewater guide for a year? Let's organize a group trip." We did not, I think it is fair to assume, react to these adventures, peculiar interests, and indulgences the way a wife or a husband would who was worried about the mortgage or getting the kids to school in the morning.

Of course it wasn't all silliness. My group of friends also came together to tackle group projects such as painting a living room, critiquing someone's rough cut of a documentary, or caring for someone who had fallen ill. We moved each other's furniture, talked each other through breakups, and attended each other's parents' funerals. Those who had money loaned it to those who didn't. Everything we owned, from books to tools to furniture to cars, was shared, or loaned or given away on an ongoing basis. When someone was out of work, we got on the phone and made networking calls on their behalf. Jen, the lawyer, went to bat for us when we got in minor scrapes with the law. The writers in the group helped others compose their grad school admission essays. Nik and Larry, who were good with their hands, could be counted on when we needed something fixed or built. Thia would cook us meals when we were down or hurt.

But noting that the activities we engaged in included the selfless (caring for a sick friend) as well as the self-absorbed (donning costumes and going to Vegas) seemed to miss a key point. I began to believe that the moral value of our lives was not in the nature of the activities we engaged in but in the friendships and group support that existed in and around them. Perhaps it was the pervasiveness of this goodwill and support (regardless of how it was ultimately employed) that was the most meaningful thing we were accomplishing with our unparalleled freedom.

Most of what we did together, after all, fell into the broad middle ground between the altruistic and the ridiculous. We shared food together, for instance, not only on every Tuesday night at the Rite Spot Cafe but in a constant series of impromptu dinners and barbecues. We played softball together. We constantly kept track of each other in a never-ending e-mail thread. On an average week, among my group of twenty-five friends, there were hundreds of one-to-one e-mails, a dozen group e-mails, and perhaps fifty phone calls exchanged. I couldn't vouch for any deep meaning in any of these communications or activities, but I could tell you that the subtext of almost all of them was a clear message of solidarity. That repeated message, from the group to the individual, was "We're on your side."

Generations may be judged by their epic battles or their grand contributions to the history of humanity, but individuals, for the most part, are judged on the sum of smaller deeds. This was easy to see within the context of families but harder to see within the context of friendships. To be an honorable spouse or a good father or mother seldom required heroics, but rather the steady demonstration of love, attention, and support. We judged fathers and mothers on whether they ate with their children, attended their games, and volunteered at their schools. No one asked whether a given family activity was morally good in and of itself; it was the love expressed during that activity that carried the meaning. Yet somehow the small things we did with and for our friends lacked the moral meaning those same acts might have in the context of a family. Cooking dinner and sharing time with one's children seemed like the act of someone who was living a good life. The act of cooking dinner for one's single friends did not carry the same weight. We seemed to lack the social narrative for how small good deeds shared among friends might be the central activity in praiseworthy lives.

What if we judged ourselves within the context of the affection and support we gave our group of friends? Would we seem less "apathetic" and "out for ourselves?"

Why You Wouldn't Have Understood

I imagine what an outsider would have thought having seen us gathered in the dirt on the Black Rock Desert, or having dinner at the Rite Spot Cafe on a Tuesday night, or that morning in my living room when Larry was planning our day. It would have been easy to perceive nothing more than a group of people hanging out or goofing off. It would have been impossible from a distance to tell who worked with whom, which of us were roommates, or who was sleeping together. It would be impossible to fathom the depth of friendships that spanned a decade or the extent to which the group occupied the mental lives of its individual members. Looking at my group, an outsider wouldn't have given it a second thought. How could it be important, this group of people sharing in each other's company? Which is to say that almost every activity we engaged in over those years belied my group's true meaning.

And here's the thing: Moments like these in my life were not merely common; they were constant. That is not to say that there was always a group of people in my living room in the midst of doing kind things for each other, or that I was always at a dinner party or on a group trip, but rather that the feeling elicited at such moments was almost always with me during those years. After more than a decade, my sense of living as a single person in a modern American city was that of belonging to an intensely loyal community of people.

Chapter 2

UNDERSTANDING THE URBAN TRIBE

Flush with the idea that I had discovered in my urban tribe something true about my generation, I rushed the idea into print. I knew that speed from idea to "idea piece" was essential in the magazine business and that it would be risky to hold on to a notion for the amount of time it would take to understand it. Among magazine writers, ideas spread in the same untraceable but maddeningly swift manner a flu spreads through the general population. If I waited too long, someone else was going to come down with my idea.

Fear of being beaten to the punch was not the only reason I worked quickly. I was also anxious to share the idea, because it seemed like good news. The idea that my group of friends comprised more than the sum of the parts represented a dawning realization that my life, which had so often felt like a talentless, improvisational dance, might have more of a structure than I had perceived. To be in your thirties and still be feeling your way along, still figuring things out, was sad and disconcerting, so I held tenaciously to any notion that suggested my life had momentum.

Unfortunately, in my haste to share the idea, I got some things wrong. Writing for the esteemed *New York Times Magazine*, I described the urban tribe as "a tight group, with unspoken roles and hierarchies, whose members thought of each other as 'us' and the rest of the world as 'them.'" I was soon to learn that this summary was fundamentally inaccurate. Of course, I had my reasons for making this mistake. Under deadline, I was straining to answer a critical question that everyone I knew, including my editors, kept asking me, namely: How are these groups of friends different from the groups of friends that people have at every other point in their lives? My sense was that these groups were more important to the yet-to-be-marrieds, but to write "These groups are more important" was to be so vague as to be meaningless. So, instead, I went about making the case that these tribes were special because the boundaries of the group were barbed-wired, almost cultish, in their rigidity. Claiming that these groups were closed and inwardly focused systems convinced my editors that these "urban tribes" were distinct, newsworthy, and worth some ink in their magazine.

But *were* these urban tribes so rigid? Were they like self-sufficient platoons of urban commandos – the Delta Force of friendships? No, they were something different entirely. I was politely alerted to my mistakes by the hundreds of people who e-mailed me after I had compounded this error by repeating it on *Good Morning America*. My correspondents had no interest in molding their lives into the narrow confines of a "thought piece" or a television sound bite. Although they recognized something familiar in my description of the urban tribe, the ones they described in their lives were only rarely tight-knit groups who saw the rest of the world as "them." They were often apologetic about this. "My groups may not fit into your definition of an 'urban tribe,'" one such respondent wrote, "but I'd like to tell you about it anyway." I began to realize that something much more complex was going on than the simple thing I described.

Through the Internet, my article on tribes had been shared from friend to friend around the world. Although most of the people who contacted me were from the United States, people e-mailed me to tell me about their tribes in India, England, Australia, Canada, and even Karachi. Many of my correspondents expressed surprise that other people were living like they were, in small societies formed by friendships and mutual interests. This surprise seemed odd at first, given that popular culture in the United States had clearly tapped the trend with sitcoms such as *Seinfeld* and *Friends*. Despite often identifying with these shows, many who wrote me said that until they read the article, they believed their lives were unique or out of the ordinary.

Because there were things about tribes that made them hard to see from the outside, they were illusive as a national trend. Tribes did not have membership rolls or official meetings. No parent or mentor had taught or encouraged the formation of these groups. No organization sponsored the national convention of urban tribes. There was no money to be made in their promotion. This sort of group behavior didn't appear to be learned (the way we learned the rules of a classroom or a church). Whatever forces created urban tribes seemed not to come out of a conscious, directed process. No one put on a New Year's resolution list, "This year, create urban tribe." Because there was no recognized social trend toward this behavior, the sensation of being in such a social entity was singular. "We thought we were the only ones" was a common refrain of my correspondents.

Sometimes they were even hard to see from the inside. At least a dozen people wrote to say that they hadn't even perceived their own tribe until they heard me describing mine. Was it possible that a group could grow so organically in the lives of its members that it could have escaped their own notice?

Learning of My Various Mistakes

To be honest, this was the second question that presented itself to me. The first and more troubling question was whether the "urban tribes" people were describing to me were analogous at all. If I had been wrong when I described these groups as tight-knit and us-versus-them, what were their meaningful similarities? As I read descriptions of tribes across the country, at first all I could see were the differences.

It became clear immediately, for instance, that there were few similarities between these groups when it came to cultural styles or interests. In the past, urban tribes might have been common among artists, gays, lesbians, bohemians, or hippies, but today it seemed that no countercultural credentials were necessary. Tribes were as likely to be made up of ultimate-Frisbee-playing MBAs from Boston as country-music aficionados from Austin, Texas. There was a group of aspiring comics in Chicago and a high-flying set of young businesspeople in London. There were dreadlocked ex-Deadheads, Ecstasy-taking rave partyers, and groups of young people who wore zoot suits and danced the lindy hop. Phil wrote me from Moncton, Canada, to tell me that his tribe, composed of members of the Society of Creative Anachronists, met to dress in full body armor and role-play characters from medieval Europe. Kimber's group in Chicago formed around a "well-respected and well-known" klezmer band.

While some urban tribes began through specific activities or pre-existing friendships, for most it was a puzzle to figure out why or how they had formed into a group. Many people who wanted to tell me about their tribes had trouble tracing the origins. The beginnings of tribes often seemed to be happenstance – roommate ads answered or acquaintances struck up in cafés. "Outsiders who see our tight bond often ask us, 'How did you all meet?'" wrote Kevin from Dallas. "It's difficult to answer because there was no specific circumstances that led to the formation of our tribe. We became friends through a variety of connections, such as friends of friends. Somehow we were magnetically drawn to each other." Nicole from San Francisco wrote of her ten-person group: "It began ten years ago through an initial pairing of one set of roommates. Those two roommates became best friends and moved to a new city together. Gradually new friends were brought into the group and new boyfriends and girlfriends were begrudgingly accepted into the group as well. There was a very delicate thread that connected us together."

Others also reported that the strength of the bond within the group could not be adequately explained through either the connections that brought them together in the first place or any shared interests or avocations. "No activity or trait defines us," Chuck from Cleveland wrote after I asked him what was unique about his group. "It's just a wonderful collection of individuals who genuinely care about each other. We ourselves are the only cool thing." Groups like Chuck's appeared to exist for no particular reason. Membership in the tribe was often the only common interest and the only relevant shared history among the members.

Those who wrote to tell me about their tribes were nearly all college educated. I had predicted this, because the marriage delay was greatest among people who stayed in school longer, especially those who went for postgraduate degrees and the demanding careers that lead from them. It made sense to me that the more time one spent outside a traditional family, the more likely it was that one would form a social entity to take its place.

In general the groups that formed from college (or sometimes high school) friendships tended to be more demographically uniform in age, race, and income. The groups that formed later, during the swirl of adult city life, could sometime match the remarkable diversity of those communities. Chris, a graphic designer in L.A., marveled at his group's mix. "When we go out to dinner we look like the UN," he wrote of his group of fifteen. "There are blacks, Italians, Thais, Filipinos, Mexicans, Colombians, Jews, Indians. Nobody seems to care about anyone else's background."

"We have Catholics, Jews, Hindus, atheists, Unitarians, socialists, liberals, Republicans, and Libertarians," wrote Jamie of his group of twenty-five members in Washington, D.C. "We lack a lot of socio-economic diversity but are internally varied in most other ways."

Christi wrote similarly of her New York group of twelve: "Our group is diverse religiously, sexually, occupationally, and physically. We have witches and ministers, gay and straight men and women, musicians, teachers, cops, lawyers, and bums. We are Latino, African American, Asian, and white. We have one friend who shoots insulin three times a day at the dinner table and another friend who has full-blown AIDS. We don't tolerate any intolerance."

Sizes of the groups were varied as well. Lee, from Kansas City, wrote to tell me about his tight group of four friends. Composed of three guys and one girl, his group formed when Lee and Mike both

44

pursued Jennifer, whom they met at the same time at church. After Jennifer rejected both of them romantically, the three became friends and soon adopted Mike's neighbor Chris into a constant stream of activities that included Sunday movie nights at Mike's house, doing laundry together, throwing parties, and going out on the town. Aside from church, the group members had no careers or avocations in common. Lee, at thirty-two, was a wannabe rock star working as an Internet banker. Mike was a former Navy nuclear engineer turned corporate executive. Jennifer was a sixth-grade teacher, and Chris was a ballet dancer. The group appeared to be held together in part by Mike's and Lee's initial interest in Jennifer. "We maintain a half-serious, half-spoken suspicion that Jennifer may wind up with one of us," he wrote. "When we date others, those others get a little maligned . . . Jennifer says she'll keep the three of us for herself. We've all contemplated moving in the past year, and we've all reached the same conclusion: the tribe has become too central to leave behind."

On the other end of the spectrum, people described a number of monster tribes such as Charles's group of more than one hundred in Denver. The group formed when members of two college alumni associations became friends and began holding large parties and organizing ski trips.

On the issue of intragroup dating, there also seemed to be a broad spectrum of practices. Some people told me that sex – or even flirtation – between members was not tolerated. Some groups (in particular the New York City tribes) described a fairly constant sexual play between group members. One group described itself as "the incest club," owing to their penchant for fooling around with each other. Although much of the energy for these groups appeared to come from those delaying marriage, long-term couples (married or not but usually without children) often existed happily within tribes.

It occurred to me that I might find meaningful commonalities among the tribes by examining the roles people within them took on. At first this appeared promising, for my correspondents identified dozens of roles within their tribes. Interestingly, few of my correspondents identified one person in their groups as the leader, de facto or otherwise. However, there was almost always at least one "organizer" (sometimes called "mother figure," "party planner," or "social director"), who appeared to earn this designation over time by successfully bringing people together or putting in the time to plan the logistics of trips and gatherings. Assuming this person was the chief of the tribe would be wrong. Having held the organizer's role off and on in my own tribe, I knew that from personal experience. The role of organizer commanded little special respect or privileges. If you wanted to be the one to go to the grocery store to gather food, or if you wanted to manage the e-mail list and make the phone calls to tell people where to show up, the role of organizer was yours for the taking. Perhaps you needed a small amount of leadership charisma to be an effective organizer, but for the most part the role was given to those willing to do the work. Oftentimes the organizer was simply the person with the biggest apartment or most centrally located home, where the group naturally gathered.

There was often another group member (usually but not always a woman) who acted as "advice giver" (called by some the group "therapist" or "shoulder to cry on"), who would console and counsel friends, particularly on the subject of romantic relationships. In one case this person was called "Switzerland" because he not only counseled individuals but also had a knack for smoothing rifts between members. Other roles people identified included "innovators," who came up with new projects for the group, and "assistants in charge of details," who followed the directions of the organizer. Other roles identified by those who wrote me included "comedian" and "deal negotiators," who would step forward when someone in the group needed help negotiating a promotion or a home purchase. There was "the worrier," who kept the group from doing dangerous things, and "the chaperone," who, in a slightly different manner, helped individuals make the choices they wouldn't regret the next morning. Women sometimes identified certain male friends as their "guardians" or "bodyguards," who could, usually just by their presence, ward off

46

unwanted advances or make them feel safer when exploring new areas of town or unfamiliar social situations. There was also sometimes a firebrand, or "life of the party," someone other people wanted to be around because he or she could draw people out of their shells and milk the most from social situations.

There were often two or three "children" in a group. These were not literal children, but adults who seemed always in trouble or in need. "The cynic" appeared to be a one variation of "the child." The cynic had the disgruntled demeanor of a two-year-old, and other group members seemed to enjoy spending large amounts of time trying to improve the cynic's mood. While you might think that groups would avoid such personalities, these "children" appeared to offer something of a group activity. The "child" would show up on a camping trip having managed to pack only hot chocolate mix. While such habits were exasperating, providing the "child" with food and shelter for the weekend made for a challenging, and ultimately enjoyable, group project. The organizer and the assistants in charge of details would rally and prove their acumen. This challenge was made more mean-ingful by the stories told later about the weekend. Often it was the boneheaded actions of the "children" that became the groups' most beloved stories to retell.

As I studied people's descriptions of these roles, some enticing patterns emerged. It was clear that there needed to be a certain balance between some roles. There were no groups with all cynics or, for that matter, all organizers or all advice givers. Some general ratios became apparent. The organizers, assistants in charge of details, and advice givers usually outnumbered the children and cynics by at least a four-to-one ratio. Christina from Raleigh, North Carolina, described such a balance: "Libby is the hostess. Mark always cooks huge dinners. Sylvia is the cruise director, always with an eye on the events calendar to rally the tribe to attend certain cool events. Jenny hosts annual Christmas parties. And then there's Bill, who shows up to everything with his dog and a six-pack." For every Bill, there seemed to be a need for a Jenny, Libby, Sylvia, and Mark. Any more Bills than that and gatherings tended to devolve into sordid beer-only events where someone's dog would throw up on someone else's bed.

In a more general view of roles, some people perceived stratification within their group along the lines of "alphas and betas" or "organizers and implementers." Sybil's group from Atlanta identified certain members as "heroes" and others as "sidekicks." "This was not because the 'hero' was necessarily the leader or the 'sidekick' a follower," she explained, "but rather describes the relationship of one person helping out another who is down." In this manner, "hero" could be turned into a verb, as she explained in this sentence: "When Josh is in town, he always heroes Ted, who is constantly broke."

Despite some interesting parallels, the differences between the tribes' internal structures always seemed to outweigh their similarities. It seemed that whenever a pattern emerged, it would blur and disappear upon closer examination. Try as I might, I couldn't go from one description of a tribe to another with any certainty that what I had learned about roles in the first was going to accurately describe the next. The roles taken on within tribes seemed less functions of group membership than expressions of personal character in a group setting. Melissa, twenty-three, who runs with an all-girl group of Asian Pacific Islanders in the San Francisco Bay Area, wrote: "We don't so much have roles as we have different personalities that shape our characters in the group . . . There is the bossy one, the joker, the ultra-fem, the quite-reserved, the secretive, etc. How the group works depends on the situation we're being presented with. Our personality shapes us to the role that fits the situation."

It seemed to me, however, that the fact people within tribes took on roles at all was something that made these groups of friends distinct. It appeared that taking on a role of some sort allowed each individual to effect a little extra gravity on the group. The gravity manifested by the organizers, those who took the time to pull people together, was the most obvious. But all the other roles functioned similarly. That people took on roles encouraged my suspicion that these groups were not just random collections of friends but functioning social entities.

Clustering Around the Core

There was another way these groups tended to differ from other, looser groups of friends one might have had in college or at other points in life – they had what social scientists call extremely high "clustering coefficients." This is the idea: You take all the people in your social circle and add up all the possible connections that could exist if absolutely every one of your friends had a personal relationship with everyone else in your social circle. Next you add up the number of people in your social circle that actually do have a personal relationship with someone you know. Your group's clustering coefficient is the number of people who actually know each other divided by the total number who could possibly know each other. So if you have six friends there is a possibility of a total number of fourteen connections within that group. If all fourteen connections actually exist, then you have fourteen divided by fourteen, or one. Your social circle couldn't be more clustered. If ten of those fourteen connections exist, your group has a clustering coefficient of 0.71. The closer your coefficient is to one, the more friends your friends share.

As I learned about tribes across the country, it became clear that their clustering coefficients were quite high. The individual friendships that made up these tribes could not be understood, I came to believe, outside the complexity of these interlocking friendships. Try to examine a single friendship while ignoring the other interlocking relationships the friends share, and the thing you wanted to examine might vanish. It was the high clustering coefficients that kept some of these relationships together.

For instance, there was a fellow in my group of friends whom I didn't much like. Let's call him Jacob. If you were to study our relationship on its own, it would not have sounded like a friendship at all. We did not talk on the phone or hang out, just the two of us. When we played sports together, the intensity of the competition belied our attempts to keep everything good-natured. In a basketball game I once gave him a black eye and was secretly pleased. Other people found him funny, but I did not, as his jokes were often at my expense. This was not a good friendship gone sour; it was always like this. Our history was spotted with bad moments, such as the time he put a cigarette hole in my couch and then lied about it, or the time he made a pass at my ex-girlfriend (the latter act being an obvious attempt to get back at me for the fact that I had briefly dated his ex-girlfriend).

My true relationship with Jacob could be understood only – and I mean only – through an understanding of the dozens of friendships that connected us. This didn't just explain the fact that he continually had the opportunity to be at my house to burn holes in my couch. The high clustering coefficient in my group revealed a more interesting fact. Because we were connected through so many others, I honestly considered him a friend. Sure, he burned holes in my couch, but if he didn't show up at a party, I would feel his absence and ask after him.

This was an extreme illustration of unexpected bonds that can form in highly clustered groups, but it's not an unusual one. Many people told me similar stories of maintaining ties through their tribes with people they otherwise would not have had as friends. High clustering coefficients create dense groups that bond friendships – both friend-ships that would exist outside the groups and many more that would not. Because of intensely high clustering coefficients, friendships in tribes sometimes defy what you'd normally expect of friendships, namely, that they are always reciprocal, positive relationships which are freely entered into and relatively freely exited from. With highly clustered groups, which friendships you are bound to often becomes as much of a group decision as a personal one. (The power of the clustering coefficient is at work in families and explains why flatulent and opinionated Uncle Simon still gets invited to Thanksgiving dinner. He is not only your uncle, he is your mother's brother and your grandparents' son. He is your brothers' and sisters' uncle as well. Families usually have a clustering coefficient of one. We love Uncle Simon, not because we like him as a person but because the connec-tions between family members exert a general gravity that keeps him tightly in our orbit.)

In describing the dynamics of their groups, many people also talked of tight "core groups" of four to twelve who were surrounded by "affiliate members," "stragglers," or "outliers" who might double or triple the size of the core group. Sometimes groups had ways of clearly stating who was a core member and who was not. Often this communication took the form of who was invited to certain events. Frieda from Oakland described how her group's weekly dinners were structured to delineate between core members and affiliates. The group met every Thursday night for dinner, but the first three Thursdays in a month were "powwow nights" that were reserved for the tribe's core dozen. The last Thursday was "Fiesta Night," when outlying members and other guests and new acquaintances were encouraged to join in.

Karla from Portland, Oregon, also described this dynamic. Her core group of lesbian friends formed out of a larger social circle a few years before, when she and seven other women all found themselves recently broken up or otherwise outside long-term relationships. They formed a softball team that summer and in the winter established a monthly poker night. At first there were some flirtations between the eight, but that was soon put aside as the importance of the interlocking friendships increased. "Initially, there were a few crushes," Karla wrote. "Soon, however, we all felt like it would be too weird to date within the group. We wanted no jealousy and no chance of any of us having to choose sides. We wanted to avoid the chaos within the group if something didn't work out."

Seeing the stability and emotional support that this group of eight offered, they soon made a rule that no significant others would be allowed to come to poker night. The larger group of about two dozen women remained accessible to new girlfriends and to others, but the core poker group was all but closed. "New people are easily accepted into the larger group. All they have to do is be nice and not detectably psychotic and they can hang out with us at parties and when we go dancing," she wrote. "However, acceptance into our poker group is very, very difficult. I know this sounds crazy but poker night is sacred to us."

Karla's description was slightly anomalous. As others described it, even the core membership of a tribe could change over the course of a year or two. In terms of how membership ebbed and flowed, these groups were not cultish in the least. In fact, they seemed uniquely designed to assimilate new members and to create social situations during which new people could be mixed in with older members. What kept the clustering coefficient high was that new people would almost immediately meet all other members of the group. Over time, most of these groups appeared to have extremely porous borders, with people joining and drifting away frequently. Janice, twenty-two, a part of a thriving Oakland tribe of technoheads, learned that at the outer edges of her group, "most people are not 'forevers.' Most people come to teach us and learn from us and off they go."

Taken as a whole, these were clearly not the us-versus-them tight-knit groups I had first described. As I saw my mistake, I also realized I fumbled a chance to correct it before the *New York Times Magazine* piece hit the presses. In an uncomfortable turn of events, the magazine asked to photograph my tribe to use with my idea piece. This led to the obvious question of whom I should include in the picture of "my tribe." I found that starting the list was easy – there were six or so people that simply had to be in the picture. But more quickly than I'd thought, I began to have doubts about who else to invite. There were a couple of people I had known through the group for years who seemed to have recently been drifting away. There was one woman who had been involved in many sexual imbroglios within the group, and I was weary of the emotional tempests that followed her around. There was the ex-girlfriend of one of the longtime members, whose membership in the group was currently in question. There was another friend who had recently been excluded from some gatherings because she had started to date someone whom the group universally didn't like. There were a few people who had recently begun joining in on group events whom I liked very much but who hardly had the history with us to qualify as tribe members. There were also a couple of new boyfriends and girlfriends who had been closely involved with the group but would not be counted as part of it outside their romantic affiliations.

In the end, I called the six core members and then I went back to a recent group e-mail list, hit "Reply All," inviting everyone else, and left it to chance as to who was going to show up. Did the resulting picture represent the urban tribe? Well, certainly not as I described it in the article that ran below it. How could such a haphazard gathering represent a "tight-knit group" that thought of each other as "us" and the rest of the world as "them"?

In terms of what I was learning about tribes from others, however, the act of bringing these people together for the photo (inviting a core group and then including a outlying ring of others based on their history with the group, their romantic affiliations, or their potential to be friends in the future) was a closer expression of the truth of these groups than I had managed to achieve in the article. In general, my correspondents came much closer to the complicated truth than I had – not only about the phenomenon in general but also about my experience in particular.

Hope in a Catchphrase

Given how wrong I had gotten the idea in the first place, I had to wonder why people had taken the time to tell me their stories. In the end, I had given them little more than the preciously coined phrase "urban tribes." But that was something. It appeared to me that those living through this unprecedented stretch of time outside of a family were starving for the slenderest notion that might begin to describe their lives. They even seemed to be excited to learn that the U.S. Census had labeled them the "never-marrieds." "Urban tribe," "never-marrieds" – being part of any group seemed better than the alternative, which was the feeling of being alone in limbo, of being stuck without a shared story for their lives.

Once they understood that they were part of a larger demographic group of people who were all facing similar situations, they were excited to take a new look at their lives with an eye to what was there, as opposed to focusing on what was missing. Once encouraged to do this, they found at least one thing to be proud of: Many had created loyal groups of friends, friends who supported and cared for each other in the dizzying swirl of their young-adult city lives. Not being married at thirty or thirty-five or forty suddenly seemed less of a failure. But given all the variation I had discovered in the style, structure, and size of these groups, I still wondered whether they had any shared meaning.

The most consistent commonality I found was not in the description of these groups but in my reaction to them: I generally liked the people who wrote or phoned me to tell me about their tribes. To say that these people expressed deep concern for the well-being of their friends would be putting it far too mildly. I knew that loyalty to one's friends was not a characteristic exclusive to my demographic group, but as I learned more about these groups of friends, I sensed something in the energy and depth of their devotion that seemed unique.

In a few cases the group's good deeds spoke to the power of having such a force in one's life. Many tribes told me that they had pooled money to send an individual member on vacation or to fly a member who had moved away from home back for a visit. Also common was the spirit of barn raising, by which groups would pitch in to build decks, paint rooms, or remodel each other's houses. Tribes were also adept at quickly mobilizing to come to the aid of individual members in acute distress. People told stories of staying in shifts at a friend's house to ward off the return of abusive boyfriends. One group in San Francisco gathered several thousand dollars to help pay the medical bills of one of their members who went through a particularly difficult pregnancy. When a parent died, tribes would rally and give support to the bereaved, often attending the funeral. A number of groups described helping individual members pay rent while they were between jobs, whether they were laid off, sick, or injured. A woman from Tempe, Arizona, wrote to tell me how a tribe, which formed from a shared interest in belly dancing, had come to the rescue of one of its members who had to move out of her apartment because of a sadistic landlord. They arrived on the scene outfitted in their dance skirts, beads, and turbans, befuddling the landlord with their outrageous attire.

"We're like a bunch of Amish people," wrote Karen of her Seattle group. "We're always helping each other out, painting houses, planting grass, fixing heaters, lending cars."

Mostly, however, the meaning of what happened in these tribes appeared not to be in their ability to pull off grand or heroic acts. As I had discovered in my own life, the meaning of these groups existed more in the combined weight of smaller favors, routines, and rituals. These tribes provided structure for members' lives in the form of annual events and parties as well as other more frequent rituals. Like my own, many groups ate weekly dinners together. There were book groups, poker nights, wine tastings, and cocktail hours, weekly sporting events, and gatherings to watch television shows such as *Sex in the City*, *Survivor*, or *The Sopranos*. Many groups rented holiday houses together or had one weekend each year reserved to go camping. The South by Southwest music festival, ultimate-Frisbee tournaments, the New Orleans Jazz Festival, Burning Man, and various carnivals were popular annual group outings. Some birthdays (or clusters of birthdays) became annual events as well. One tribe of ten from New York internally published a yearly calendar, which included the birthdays of all the members and reminders of the days reserved for the group's other annual events.

There were also yearly rituals that were made up out of the group's history. One woman in Philadelphia wrote to tell me that her group has semiannual "interesting women meetings." These were potluck woman-only dinners in which new acquaintances could be introduced to the group. In a similar vein, thirty-three-year-old Maschelle from Charleston, West Virginia, wrote that her group held an annual "Diva/Goddess Party," which was a combination talent show and discussion of current women's issues. Lisa's group of ten girls in London took regular trips to Sheffield, where most of them had gone to college.

Tribes sometimes hijacked holidays from traditional families. These tended not to be the top-tier holidays such as Christmas or Thanksgiving, when many people still traveled to their hometowns to celebrate with parents and siblings (although members of tribes who, for a variety of reasons, could not leave town often gathered for small "orphan Thanksgivings" or "orphan Christmases"). Long weekends such as Memorial Day and Labor Day were often reserved for tribe trips or parties. New Year's Eve in particular, which appeared to be the most common tribe celebration, typically grew more elaborate from year to year. Tribe members who had moved away from the home base of their group would often travel great distances to celebrate New Year's with their old comrades.

All of these annual, monthly, and weekly events could pack a social schedule. Lisa, from New York City, who, along with her roommate/ best friend, organized events for a large tribe of sixty people, described their remarkably crowded calendar. They had yearly trips to the jazz festival in New Orleans, a Thanksgiving ski trip, Fourth of July in Las Vegas, and a semiannual gathering for volleyball tournaments held in Clearwater, Florida. On a monthly basis they held one "women's summit" dinner and one coed party. On a weekly basis some portion of the group gathered for volleyball (on Tuesdays), football (on Sundays), and swing dancing (on Wednesdays).

The scheduled or ritualized events were only the beginning of the tribes' social life. Lisa and others described a constant stream of impromptu gatherings, sometimes to celebrate successes such as promotions or new apartments and sometimes for no reason at all. E-mail group lists made gathering at least part of the group as easy as writing a short note and tapping "Send." Tribe members described spending time with other members as often as once a day. People wrote of the self-confidence and sense of inclusion that came from having a place to go on the weekend and friendly messages on their answering machines at the end of the day.

Heather, from Fremont, California, described the pervasiveness of the tribe's presence in the lives of its members. Her group, most of whom originally met working at a Starbucks, was a remarkable menagerie consisting of blacks, whites, and Hispanics, gays and straights, as well as immigrants from Germany, Afghanistan, Korea, and Portugal. "Because of the diverse nature of our group we have a range of opinions on the issues of the day," Heather wrote. "But we are like family. We give each other rides to the airport, we cover each other's shifts, we care for those who get sick and give each other money when we're in a pinch. We feed each other – every meal I eat is with at least one member of this group – and we cut each other's hair."

On the surface, each one of the many activities that these people described might not seem very significant, and many of them (meeting to watch television or play poker) could be dismissed as banal forms of socializing. Taken in concert, however, they all seemed to be part of the music of devotion. My correspondents didn't make the case that their activities were necessarily important or meaningful. It was the social momentum that they prized – and it seemed not to matter whether it was directed toward the silly or the serious. The social momentum that gathered people for a party one month would be the same energy that led them to travel across two states to attend a friend's parent's funeral the next.

In the end, my description of the tribe as "tight-knit" and "us-versus-them" was only half a mistake. While my sources let me in on the fact that these tribes were quite fluid in their membership, they recognized the emotional truth of what I was trying to get at. Despite changing membership, at any given moment in time these groups could give the *feeling* of exclusivity, of being clearly defined.

At first this seemed like something of a paradox: How could these constantly changing groups provide the sensation that they were tight-knit? The answer came from looking at other, more formal long-standing groups. Sports teams, fraternities, or civic groups, for instance, might have significantly different memberships each year, but they also maintained the sense that they were a single entity by maintaining a history of the group – a history into which new members could easily be written. It appeared that urban tribes also maintained a narrative momentum, which gave meaning to the group over time even though the composition of the group might change. When new members were included on, say, a tribe's annual Memorial Day camping trip to the Blue Ridge Mountains, those new members immediately became part of the larger narrative of the tribe. By going on one trip, they were woven into the group's story, which included all the trips the group had taken. It was possible, then, for groups to seem consistent and trustworthy even with members coming and going over time. That the meaning and momentum of an urban tribe might exist outside the combined strength of the individual friendships – that the tribe might have a life of its own – was one distinction these groups had from groups of friends one might have at other points in life.

"The Group"

Even as the similarities between tribes came to light, that second question began to gnaw at me: If these groups were similar, why had there been so little public recognition of them?

Among the descriptions of tribes from across the country and around the world, I received nearly a dozen messages from a single vibrant tribe in Philadelphia. Calling themselves simply "the group," or alternatively "our group," they had forty-four semiofficial members listed on their Web site but a mass e-mail list that included another twenty names. Most of the group's members were around thirty but ages ranged from twenty-four to forty. It was equally split between men and women, who had a wide range of careers. They were lawyers, nonprofit administrators, health care workers, and business consultants. Many were active in the local chamber of commerce through an affiliate group called the Young Professionals Network, which encourages philanthropy and civic participation in the city's young adults. The accepted ethos of the group was that new friends and acquaintances – and anyone else who came into the group's orbit – should be embraced, which probably accounted for its unusually large size.

"The group" kept its members busy. The Web site calendar for the group was packed with events. On a weekly basis there were happy hours, karaoke nights, soccer and volleyball games. There was an endless series of birthday parties and monthly "orphan Sunday dinners," which sprang out of the "orphan holiday dinners" held for those who couldn't easily travel home to family. Taken together, it was a daunting series of social events. As one member wrote me, "Should I choose, I could have something to do with the group every night."

The number of people and events created something of a social juggernaut. The group was nothing more or less than "a way of life," wrote a female member. Friends and family outside the group were often confused and even put off by the tribe's impact on the lives of the members. "People who I tell about the group seem to have a hard time understanding what it is – they seem to have nothing similar to compare it with," one male group member told me. "People have asked me if it's a cult or how it's possible to have fifty friends. Some people even seem to feel sorry for me, as if I have some kind of pseudo family that is pathetic."

Among the spectrum of urban tribes I was learning about, this group in Philadelphia had more structure and was more self-consciously an entity than most – a fact that was likely due to the existence of the Web site. Although they prided themselves on being open to new people, inclusion on the group's Web site conferred de facto membership. And while the tribe had begun with friendships formed in at college, several members even dated the "official" start of the group with the launching of the site.

Steve, who ran the Web site and the main e-mail distribution list, found himself in the position of group "gatekeeper." Given the group's ethos of inclusion, gatekeeper was not a position of much power in terms of shaping the group. If someone asked him to include a friend on the distribution list, he would rarely fail to do so. While he was proud that no one had ever been pulled off the list or kicked out of the group, he was frank that this sometimes led to difficulties. "The fact that we never kick anyone out can be a problem," he told me. "There are some people in the group who are not very well liked, but there is no process to get them out of the group. They keep showing up at events, making the events less enjoyable."

As with other jumbo tribes, some members described smaller groups forming within the larger group. Jackie, a twenty-five-year-old management consultant, described the tribe as having three dozen "central members" with a few dozen more peripheral characters. From her personal perspective, however, there was a group of ten that composed her close friends. The larger group, in part, provided a comfortable social setting for the smaller group of her strongest friendships. This is not to say that Jackie considered the rest of the tribe wallpaper. "I'm closer with some than others," she told me, "but I would have to say that any of them would be there for me if I needed them and I would be there for them."

But when I asked Jackie further about these groups within groups, it became clear that the large tribe had reached something of a critical mass. "Over the last few months the dynamics of our group have definitely changed," she told me. "It is no longer questioned if you are not invited somewhere. The borders of the subgroups are understood. We've had a couple of birthday dinners over the last few weeks in which there were only ten or fifteen of us invited. And there was a holiday party this past weekend that myself and most of my group of close friends were not invited to."

There were a couple of people who spent time trying to keep the larger group intact. They were called "the diplomats" and could be counted on to hold events where everyone was included and spend time soothing hurt feelings when someone had felt left out. Group cohesion did not rest entirely on the shoulders of the diplomats, however, as all group members were allowed to use the Web site and group distribution list to sponsor gatherings or encourage members to attend public events. Some noted that a few members of the group cared little for the large group events and were pleased that the borders of the subgroups were becoming more defined.

Others saw the formation of groups within groups as part of the unavoidable process during which certain sets of friendships became stronger over time, creating loyalties that eventually became stronger than the loyalty to the group as a whole. "I see the interaction as similar to a fraternity I was in at Penn State," one tribe member told me. "You start out as a freshman and you are all excited to participate. As you get older, your interaction is more limited to those you know and finally when you are ready to graduate, you break off and pretty much hang out with your close friends mostly, but see the overall group once in a while."

It was difficult to tell how the group affected the romantic lives of its members. Steve, who admitted to being a little shy around women, said he had more confidence in social situations in which he might meet women because he could count on having friends from the group there to support him. "Also, having a big group of friends makes you more attractive to the women you meet," he said, although it was unclear to me whether he knew this to be true or simply hoped it was.

In general, it was far from clear whether the group helped or hindered romantic endeavors. Several people, for instance, described difficulties in bringing new romantic partners into the tribe. "It can be strange to date someone who is not part of the group," wrote one woman member. "You never know if you want to bring them around or if you want to keep them separate. If you bring them around too much, they become a part of the group, so you have to put some thought into that decision." Recently, one of the women members brought a new flame to several group events and was disturbed at how readily he was accepted. "We all LOVED him," wrote one woman who witnessed the dynamic. "He was the nicest guy ever and we all started inviting him places personally, which didn't sit well with the group member he was dating. As we explained to her, she shouldn't have brought him around so soon."

More difficult still was the gauntlet of dating within the group. Even mild flirtations were noticed and discussed. Everyone felt invested in these couplings, because everyone understood that an intragroup relationship might portend group conflict if the relationship turned sour. Recently, one of the male group members dated a series of women in the group. While none of these relationships overlapped in time, there was inevitable jealousy and hard feelings. For this reason, some of the female members within the tribe said they actively discouraged such casual intratribal dating. Couples who had proved that they were long-term were more readily accepted. There were currently no fewer than five engagements within the group – a fact that most expressed excitement about.

The tribe seemed intensely interested in the love lives of its individual members. The unspoken rule appeared to be: Don't date someone within the group or bring a new love interest around unless you think it might be the real thing. As Jackie wrote, before dating within the group or bringing someone in from outside "you really have to know that the person is sticking around in your life for a while."

Fiesta in Philly

Figuring that the only way to understand "the group" was to take a look at it in person, I flew to Philadelphia after Gordon, the group's main organizer of events, was kind enough to invite me to the annual Cinco de Mayo fiesta. When I showed up at the two-bedroom apartment that Gordon shared with his fiancée, Goldie, the party was just warming up. Most people were hanging out in the kitchen, where Goldie was preparing a variety of Mexican-themed hors d'oeuvres.

From their looks, most of the members of "the group" were not the homecoming queens or football quarterbacks of their high schools. I imagined that, like me, they might have been found in more nerdish and marginalized extracurriculars, such as the debate team or the French club or the staff of the school newspaper. They were gracious and affable in a disarming yet unsuave manner that made me think that they had recently discovered their social acumen. Steve, the Web master, told me that he, like many other group members, "had few friends before joining the group."

As the party went on, I tried to learn what I could of how this tribe functioned, but I found it was more difficult than I had imagined. Even from my vantage point – literally in the midst of a tribal gathering – the bonds and borders of the group were largely invisible.

Here's what I could see from my position in the corner of the room at the high point of the party. There were more than fifty people packed into Gordon and Goldie's plainly appointed apartment. Most everybody was in their early thirties and casually dressed. Racially the group was largely white and Asian. (I saw no Hispanics despite – or possibly because of – the theme of the event.) From the warmth of the greetings and general liveliness of the discussions, I could tell that most of these people knew each other – but that was about all I could discern. Had not a number of the group's members described its workings ahead of time, it would not have been at all clear from looking at it that this gathering constituted a long-standing tribe.

Whatever group structure might exist in the minds of the members, there was little hierarchy visible or roles evident in the event. Neither Gordon nor anyone else addressed the group as a whole. (The only group activity all night was the breaking of the piñata, which took less than five minutes.) All that was going on was small sets of three or four people leaning close to each other to be heard over the blasting salsa music. There was no way to distinguish those who had been to many of the group events from those who might have been meeting the group for the first time. I had flown across the country to "see" another urban tribe, but I discovered that even in its midst, the shape of the tribe was hidden from me. Not only did these groups not have any outward apparatus (no membership rolls or official meetings), they were virtually invisible to an observer.

Gordon, who was genuinely trying to make me feel included, kept introducing me to small groups of people and then moving away to pour drinks or welcome new arrivals. Each time this happened, the group would attempt to include me for a time in the conversation. They'd ask questions about who I was and why I was there. As soon as they felt like they had made a gracious attempt to include me, the topic of the conversation turned back to what it had been before I arrived: chitchat and gossip about their lives and those of their mutual friends. They talked about their challenges, disgruntlements, or successes at work. They shared information about the best places to buy up-and-coming property in the area and which shops had the best clothes or produce. Mostly, they passed on news of other friends – particularly if that news had to do with their love lives.

Sometimes the group would try to give me a little background on the people they were talking about, but these details failed to make the gossip interesting to me. Unable to follow or muster much interest in these stories, I would listen for a time and then find an excuse to step away. A little while later, Gordon would find me sitting alone on the couch and throw me into another group of two or three and the scene would repeat itself. Eventually, I'd end up shuffling my feet, listening to gossip about people I didn't know. Even with the protective shield of being "the reporter," it was hard to avoid the feeling of being the stray hyena circling the pack. When I found myself talking with groups of men, I noticed I took a slightly submissive posture, slumping my shoulders slightly and glancing at the floor.

As the party continued, I began to wonder whether I was feeling as close to these people as I thought I would. Some of the men seemed a little puff-chested and showed up wearing expensive leather jackets of a style that would be pretentious among my group back in San Francisco. The women wore more makeup and had hair that was more carefully styled than I was accustomed to seeing on women my age in San Francisco. The ubiquity of the party's "theme" – the salsa music, the Mexican finger food, the tequila drinks, and the obligatory piñata – seemed a little high-schoolish.

This was nothing like my group in San Francisco, I found myself thinking. Sure, we had theme parties too. We had even held Cinco de Mayo fiestas. But there was a world of difference. Our theme parties had so much more irony than this cookbook "fiesta." We went so much more over the top with our themes – including Frito chips and wide-brim sombreros – that nobody could conclude that we were seriously trying to coopt Hispanic culture. And the conversations among my friends at home were certainly more insightful and filled with meaning.

At least I thought they were. But as I recalled conversations from my tribe's recent events, I had the uncomfortable realization that they were not just similar to those here in Philadelphia, they were nearly identical in subject matter. Truth be told, everything about this party was familiar, especially the way this group liked to separate off into small clusters of three and four people and gossip about the lives of mutual friends.

The leather jackets, the permed and highlighted hair, and the particular style of this fiesta were hardly meaningful differences. Being an outsider, however, I found it necessary to find them lacking. I was judging these genuinely kind people with such paltry evidence for the simple reason that in this situation they were fundamentally uninterested in me. Those impressions, as defensive and childish as they were, proved instructive. Over e-mail and the telephone, I had found it quite easy to identify with these people. However, at that party, where it was clear that I was not part of the group, I discovered a need to find fault.

My brief immersion in "the group" showed me that these groups weren't only hard to see, they were hard to *feel* as well. While I understood the warmth and support my group provided me, it was impossible to expect that feeling to be apparent to an outsider visiting for a couple of days. The social gravity that tribes exerted on members seemed to defy the understanding of those outside the group.

Gossip and Grooming

Or maybe I had just missed seeing the obvious. A few months after visiting the group in Philadelphia, I came across the work of Robin Dunbar, a professor of biological anthropology at the University of Liverpool. Since the eighties Dunbar had been publishing papers that argued an interesting connection between the use of language and the size of groups we humans chose to socialize in. Nonhuman primates,

65

he had noted, had complex social groups that required intense social bonds between individual members. These monkey-to-monkey bonds were expressed and maintained through the act of grooming. Apparently, when one monkey pets and picks at another monkey's fur, he is expressing his solidarity with that other monkey.

For monkeys, this takes a significant amount of time and effort. The bigger the group, the more time each monkey has to spend maintaining the ties that bind. In large groups of fifty baboons or chimpanzees, for example, the animal could spend up to one fifth of its day grooming others. Obviously, there was a limit to this activity; monkeys had other things on their day planners. Dunbar theorized that it was these time constraints on grooming that limited the size of the monkey group. If too many monkeys hung out together, there wouldn't be enough time to accomplish the amount of grooming necessary to bind the group together. This could lead to monkey knife fights and general confusion as to who was on whose side.

At first it was hard to see how this might correspond to human behavior. It was only on very rare occasions that I picked the dead skin off of my friends scalps, and it certainly wasn't my preferred way to express solidarity. Dunbar's theory was that humans had replaced grooming with talking – gossipy talking in particular. The use of gossip as grooming was not, he believed, an offshoot of language but the very reason it developed in our species.

I was quick to think that Dunbar was on to something – especially when his idea was compared with an alternative theory for the development of language. Conventional wisdom was that language evolved in the context of hunting. It's certainly plausible that the first sentence was something along the lines of "Look out, there's a saber-toothed tiger behind you!" But from what I had experienced of human nature, I would have wagered all that I had on the first sentence being something like "Did you hear that Gork went out foraging with Humulok last night and didn't come home until morning?" Studies (along with my personal experience) have shown that gossip is the primary use of language in modern times, and I saw no particularly good reason why it wouldn't have started out that way.

Dunbar also believed there was a connection between the size of a species' neocortex and the amount of social interaction it could manage. The bigger the neocortex, the bigger the group. Making a ratio of the size of a monkey's neocortex to its group size, Dunbar came up with this simple equation: $\log(N) - 0.093 + 3.389 \log(CR)$ (1) ($r2=0,764$, $t34=10.35$, $p<0.0001$), where N is the mean group size and CR is the ratio of neocortex volume to the rest of the brain. I don't know what this means, either, but I take his word that if you plug in a human's neocortex volume (10006.5 cc), you'll come up with the conclusion that human group size maxes out at around 150 people.

But if apes had only enough time for the grooming that it took to maintain the bonds between fifty animals, how did humans have the time to potentially maintain bonds with 150? We had appointments in our day planners, too. The size of our groups could be bigger, Dunbar answers, because language is a more efficient way to "groom" than one-on-one physical contact. Monkeys had to groom each other while staying more or less stationary. We, however, could gossip while working out on Stairmasters and over a cell phone while driving. But most important, we could gossip *in groups*, and thereby "socially groom" two or three group members at a time. Language evolved as an efficient way to maintain the bonds of the larger groups we apparently once needed to survive and prosper.

Gossip was more efficient in another way. When three or four members of a social group get together and share information about other group members' personal relationships, they are passing along important information that allows us to know other members of the group better. Without the information transmitted through gossip, our group size would be likely be limited, because each group member would have to spend more time personally observing the behavior of every other group member.

But what was with the number 150? At first that number seemed uniquely unsatisfying – too large to account for the urban tribe groupings I was trying to document and much too small to account for cities or neighborhoods. Dunbar made it clear, however, that he was referring specifically to the *maximum* number of a group in which everybody could know everybody else at least by sight, if not by interaction. Clearly he was not describing cities, but rather groups in which an individual could have some personal and coherent relationship with all the other individuals over a period of time. Put another way, he theorized that 150 was the maximum size at which a group might maintain adherence to its rules solely through the use of peer pressure.

Dunbar took great pains to find examples of human groupings that topped out at 150. Men in armies fought most effectively when they felt a social group bond with soldiers they fought beside. History had proven, apparently, that this social bond dramatically diminished when individual fighting units exceeded 150 men. The 150 figure was not an the optimal size of human groups, but rather the maximum size of human groups – the point just before, as Dunbar put it, "complete social collapse." The optimal size of a human group would be something less than 150 and would vary depending on the demands of the particular environment and needs of group members.

Groups, he figured, would tend to oscillate around the optimal size needed for their particular environment. Successful groups – particularly those with porous borders – would inevitably grow past their optimal size and then split into daughter groups that would begin the process again. Dunbar also noted that within any group of primates – human included – not all relationships would be equal. Within the group, individuals would naturally have a few very intense emotional relationships and a larger number of less meaningful relationships. Clusters of the intense relationships would naturally form into interconnected cliques. These cliques did not work against the group cohesion but were part of the necessary internal webbing that held together large groups.

What was the optimum size for the urban tribe? There was another sized group that received only brief mention in Dunbar's works but caught my attention. He noted that on the smaller end of human groups there used to be what he called "bands" or "night camps," which were composed, on average, of thirty-seven individuals but ranged from less than a dozen to more than fifty. I began to think our apparent natural desire for a group of this size might be the impetus of modern urban tribes.

If Dunbar was right, the gossiping between small groups within the larger group I witnessed in Philadelphia was the activity at the very heart of tribes everywhere. Dunbar had even nearly predicted (through his own study of the reach of the human voice) the size of the grooming clusters I had seen. He figured that given the projection of the human voice, we would gossip in groups of 3.4 on average. I'd put the average gossiping group at the Philadelphia party at closer to 3.0 – a discrepancy likely explained by the amplified salsa music. The theory also explained why their gossip seemed unimportant to me while the gossip of my group back home was fascinating. If gossip was the act of expressing alliance membership, it would be important only to those entering or already in the group. In Philadelphia, among the group, I was neither.

Which was, I realized, another reason so many of these groups could exist without joining forces or becoming a recognized national trend: they would escape the notice of others because the very thing that bonded them – the use of gossip – was all but meaningless to those not in the group.

There was something else that Dunbar's theory made clear. He answered for me how these groupings might have formed so naturally in our lives as to escape our notice. If grouping through gossip was instinctual, then it made sense that we needed no lessons to behave in this manner. Left alone, free to choose our own path in life, these groups would naturally form around us, no blueprint necessary. We were doing what came naturally.

Chapter 3

ON FRIENDSHIP AND RISK

"I think the main purpose of our group is that it provides us with people to hang out with until we get married," Steve of the Philadelphia tribe said to me at their fiesta. He was the sort of guy who had a habit of calling it like he saw it. He clearly had no idea that he had rather bluntly stated my deepest fear about these groups: namely, that they represented nothing more than an easy holding pattern until we had the opportunity to land in the real world of marriage and family. Steve did not seem frightened by this notion, which was likely due to the fact that he was ten years younger than I. Going into a holding pattern for a few years after college was no big deal. I, however, was in my thirteenth year of living this sort of lifestyle. It was pretty depressing to consider the possibility that the only thing it amounted to was "hanging out," waiting for the marriage train to arrive.

It was clear that there was a lot of warmth in these tribes, but I still wasn't sure if, on the whole, they were having a positive influence on people's lives or somehow holding them back. Of course, everyone who told me about their groups thought the world of their friends and all the fun they had together. But just because these people attested that the tribe years were good for them didn't mean they were. People have been known to claim that all sorts of things were good for them (macrobiotic diets, law school) only to realize later that they had fooled themselves. Because we cannot see the paths we have not taken, we become, by default, advocates for the path our life is on.

For me, the overall assessment of my tribe tended to change with my moods. On days when I was feeling generally good, the matrix of these friendships seemed like the main source of energy and momentum in my life. The fact that Larry was writing a song about one of my failed relationships (entitled "The World's Saddest Girlfriend in the World") would on those days seem charming. I would count down the hours to the next group trip or get-together. On days when I was feeling down, however, the tribe and my houseful of roommates seemed like the locked box in which my life was trapped. How could I justify being in my mid-thirties and spending so much time goofing off with my friends? How could I move on and find a life partner if my friends were hovering about literally composing odes to my failed romances?

Even on the good days I sometimes worried that we all might be fooling ourselves about any deep meaning in this way of living. I avoided the television show *Friends* because it made me nervous. The show had unmistakable parallels with my life. There was the affection and support between the characters and the constant tension created by intra- and extra-tribal romantic relationships. I couldn't watch, however, because I feared another parallel: every week the show featured the same characters playing out plotlines that led nowhere. The nature of their relationships seemed to freeze the characters in a state of perpetual young-adult cluelessness.

As I continued to receive reports of tribes across the country, I began to notice a similarity in some of the descriptions. It took me a while to notice this resemblance, because the message was hidden in vague and flowery language that I tended to ignore. Take for instance this statement from Andrea in San Diego: "My group has changed me by giving me a sense of personal power and confidence that I did not wholly possess on my own," she wrote of her tribe of thirteen core members and twenty-five affiliates. "The group encourages me to remain true to myself at all times. With the sense of belonging it gives me, it is easy to take many risks in my life and to stand confidently on my own two feet."

At first I skimmed past such descriptions, because they sounded like the affirmations on the backs of the self-help books I loathed. I have a mild allergy to clichés that have to do with standing on one's own two feet or remaining true to oneself. In defining the meaning and function of urban tribes, these were exactly the sort of phrases I wanted to avoid. Although I had no doubt that testimonials like Andrea's were sincere, I only began to pay attention to them when I heard remarkably similar sentiments repeated from people across the country.

Andrea's statement sounded like an echo of this one from Leah in Monmouth Junction, New Jersey: "I've grown a lot through my tribe. I've found out more about myself, developed in areas I would not have if I weren't involved with these people. I now know what I want out of life or at least what I don't want. I know I will not settle for the wrong man or the wrong job. I have a strong source of support. I know they will tell me when I am out of line, need to change or rethink a situation – sometimes without asking for their opinion. I guess you could say that I've found myself."

A few days later I found the same sentiments expressed by Christi in New York: "I am a strong individual – very independent but I rely on my friends to be a sounding board for any issues in my life. My friends make me a better person and they expect a lot from me. They set standards and they help me live up to them. My group helps me define myself."

People seemed to believe that they were becoming themselves – that they were being allowed to express their individual natures – not despite group peer pressure but as a product of it. How, I wondered, could a group's "setting high standards" or telling you that you were "out of line" allow you to discover your individual identity?

I didn't fully understand the meaning of what these people were saying until I was searching the Web with words like "friendship," "loyalty," "meaning of," and came across Aristotle's thought on the topic. Actually, it was not Aristotle's writing I found but rather a half-dozen student papers written about Aristotle. According to these trenchant scholars (who ranged from high school students to Ph.D. candidates), Aristotle noodled a good deal on friendship. Much of what he came up with seemed fairly straightforward and unremarkable. He noted, for instance, that some friendships were based on the enjoyment of one another's company or, alternatively, on the exchange of one favor for another. But there was also a higher form of friendship, according to Aristotle, that transcended these requirements. This was "friendship in the good," and it had a very particular meaning.

Aristotle made the curious observation that our best and most caring behavior toward our friends was very similar to our best and most caring behavior toward ourselves. That is to say, sometimes we wished for a friend the same good fortune and virtue that we wished for ourself. If I respected a friend as I respected myself, my friend could be regarded, in Aristotle's thinking, as my other self.

Tying one's self-regard into the idea of friendship seemed, at first, to demean it. But, as my menagerie of scholars patiently explained, Aristotle was actually praising this form of friendship as the highest level of altruism. If I wanted a good and virtuous life for my friend as reflexively and nakedly as I wanted a good and virtuous life for myself, I was being about as genuinely generous as I could hope to be.

But there was a catch. By Aristotle's definition, before I could manage this "friendship in the good," I had to have already achieved virtue myself. What Aristotle called "virtue" we call self-respect – that internal compass that guides us toward the things that are good and meaningful in life, as opposed to the things that are just pleasurable or advantageous. Those who were self-destructive or knew only the pursuit of pleasure or had not yet figured out what was good and true in their lives could not achieve "friendship in the good." You could not wish for a friend the goodness and virtue (a.k.a. self-respect) you did not yourself possess.

Leah, Andrea, and Christi were on to Aristotle's idea that friendship was connected to self-respect, but there was a clear difference. These women were suggesting that it was not self-respect that allowed good friendships but good friendships that created a path to self-respect. These women wrote of growing into themselves – of "finding" and "defining" themselves – through the process of friendships in their tribes.

"Becoming part of a group like this, you definitely see how people perceive you," Kathy from Arlington, Virginia, told me. "I have learned a lot more about myself." It was as if they were looking to their group of friends to see a reflection of themselves and their behavior. They were gaining knowledge of themselves not by navel gazing but through seeing their reflections in their exchanges with other people. Leah, Andrea, Christi, Kathy, and Aristotle were making the case that there was something about friendships that allowed us to glimpse ourselves in the interaction.

This is not to say that friends necessarily give us the *clearest* reflection of ourselves. When I would ask people to describe their friends in their urban tribes, they would inevitably stumble over themselves to tell me how fabulous those friends were. Their friends were always "talented and smart," "charming and generous," or "adventurous and fun-loving." "Our group has the most interesting people you would ever meet," said one man from Denver. "My friends are the most talented artists and musicians I have ever come across," wrote Heather from Portland. Mary from Pittsburgh described her twenty tribe members as "wonderful, smart, loving people." Did I have such high regard for people in other groups when I met them? Inevitably I did not. This is not to say that they didn't have these qualities. As in Philadelphia, I would compare them with my own fabulous, talented, loving friends and find these strangers always lacking.

Like my correspondents, I saw an idealized version of my friends – trumpeting their strengths and minimizing their weaknesses. Often I could even see their flaws as attributes. So-and-so wasn't bossy; she was organized. Another person wasn't a depressive; he was intriguingly moody. In turn they would do the same for me: I wasn't a flake; I was a free spirit. These were not falsehoods so much as they were positive spins on our personalities and behaviors.

Because we see ourselves reflected in our friends and they see themselves reflected in us, everyone has a stake in seeing the best in each other. "My friends are creative/wonderful/loving/smart" was the text. The subtext was: "Because they are my friends, I am also creative/wonderful/loving/smart." What we saw of ourselves in the mirror of our friendships was not our true selves but our best selves.

What do I mean by "best self"? Certainly it is not the same for everyone. Our individual personalities, talents, and upbringings create our own unique "best selves." One person's best self might be an ambitious high achiever; another's might be a charming social ballerina. Another's best self might only be able to hold down a job, be kind to his cat, and pay the rent. These groups did not exist to mold people into a set group personality with equal talents or similar attributes.

But hadn't Christi said that her group "set standards" and made sure she lived up to them? Hadn't Leah said that her group told her when she was "out of line"? I came to understand that the group pressure these women described was not pressure to *conform* to the group. The "standards" Christi was talking about were particular to her friends' perception of her individual potential: Her friends had come to perceive her best self, and they expected her live up to that standard. Leah's group, similarly, could be counted on to tell her when she was out of line – not with an expectation of group behavior, but out of line with her best self.

Friendship and Risk

My correspondents often specifically linked the self-respect that came from strong friendships with the ability to take risks in their lives. "They are the only people who can make me feel totally accountable to myself," wrote Sarah, twenty-five, from Cedar Rapids. "They totally understand me and provide a space where nothing is too embarrassing or risky. It's ideal, really, because I have total freedom to take risks and yet I have a place to feel at home."

This connection seemed particularly important given the time of life the tribe years encompass. Of course there are risks to be taken at every point in life, but those in the postcollege years seemed particular in that we were often taking chances in every aspect of our lives nearly simultaneously. We had to choose and forge our careers: we had to pick our politics, our mates (eventually), and sometimes even our sexuality. Untethered from our families and outside the safety of school, we were making decisions and choosing directions that would affect the rest of our lives. The risks that we chose to take would form our adult identity. To understand this connection between friendship and risk, I needed to look no farther than my own tribe. With the support from our shared tribe, one friend of mine had recently met a remarkably difficult challenge

When I first met Nikolas he ran a small glass sculpting studio in the Mission District of San Francisco, where he molded glass vases, platters, and lamps, as well as limited-edition art pieces inspired by organic forms: the ribbing of a seashell, ripples on water, or a lick of flame. He had come into our circle after being invited to our Tuesday-night dinners by Todd and Rob, old classmates from Brown University.

After a year of consistent attendance every Tuesday, he didn't show up one night, and I asked after him. Nikolas was working late, Todd told me, then described the challenge he was up against. Nikolas had received the commission of a lifetime. He had been asked by Frank Gehry, arguably the most famous architect of our time, to create what was perhaps the largest glass lighting installation *in the world* for a high-profile building going up in the heart of reunited Berlin.

When I saw Nikolas next, it was clear he was in over his head. The lighting installation he had proposed to Gehry was to be composed of thirty-six enormous slabs of fused glass tubing, each resembling the shape of a wing and weighing hundreds of pounds. Nikolas admitted that he had never fired a piece of glass larger than a couple of feet long – teeny compared with the nine-foot behemoths he had told Gehry he could manufacture. He had only a year to create the three dozen pieces – five thousand pounds of glass in all – using materials he didn't know he could get, with technology he hadn't yet developed, through a process he could only vaguely imagine. He had to custom build a kiln as large as a moving van. He had to order two semi trucks of glass tubes and pray that the untested design of the panels and the untested technology would work. He was in for a literal trial by fire.

Nikolas did have resources. Tall and barrel-chested, he had a natural confidence that he used to win people to his side. (He had something of an endearing old-school style about his interactions with people, often addressing them with honorary titles. He always greeted me as "Dr. Watters.") Having run his own studio since he was twenty-one, Nikolas had overcome hundreds of technical challenges to discover new ways to bend and mold glass. He was used to working hard and finding creative solutions to stumbling blocks. This project would test these talents to their breaking points. It was when he reached those breaking points that he found a critical resource in the support of his friends.

Of course we all cheered him on. But this wasn't the type of help he needed. He needed those who could provide very real, substantive support. Our mutual friend Jamie was the first to step up and shoulder some of Nikolas's burden.

Critical to the project's success was figuring out how to organize the thousands of glass tubes he had purchased into the shapes he had designed. It was a tremendously complex puzzle. Each of the thirty-six pieces was formed with hundreds of tubes of different lengths and diameters. In order to be structurally sound, the outside of each tube had to touch another tube in no less than three points. In addition, Nicolas had a limited supply of each tube, so he simultaneously had to know exactly where each tube went and how much he had to have left.

Jamie, whom Nikolas had also known from Brown and who was part of our extended San Francisco tribe, happened to be a budding expert in computer-modeling complex phenomena. After talking over the problem with Nikolas, he began to create a Java-based computer program that would translate the shapes into a precise map of how the tubes should be stacked together. They dubbed the program "the Gerbilator."

Jamie was far from alone in offering help. Nik's friend Christian, who was an architect, helped design a huge loft in the studio that was used to store the tons of tubing. Other friends provided support where they could. They dropped by his studio late at night to bring him dinner and brought him breakfast when they knew he had been up all night. His friend John, a documentary filmmaker, volunteered his time to videotape the project as it evolved. My roommate Larry needed work, so Nikolas hired him as a gofer and crate builder for the project. I wrote a piece for a local magazine trumpeting the project and Nikolas's talents.

A number of people began to routinely show up on weekends and pitch in where they could. "Some of my favorite memories of the project were when I had a whole group of friends there on a weekend," Nikolas said. "We would turn up the music and drink beer and clean the pieces of the chandelier."

Of course, relying on friends in these ways was a tricky thing. When his friends pitched in, Nikolas had to be at once their boss and the grateful recipient of their generosity. The more difficult and integral the task, the harder it was to find that balance. Jamie, in particular, didn't act anything like an employee. "At times he was a really tough person to have help me out," remembered Nikolas. "He's brilliant, but he's also a hard-ass, arrogant fucker. There were times when he was just stupefied by my idiocy and he didn't think twice about telling me so. His attitude was 'Listen up, sculptor boy, this is the way we're going to do it.' "

There was some quid pro quo in these favors. Nikolas was paying Larry for his time, for instance. He also hired Jamie's young cousin. But in large part the help simply flowed Nikolas's way, without him even needing to ask. "At the time it was interesting how much I just assumed the help would be there," Nikolas told me. "Now that I look back and add all the time and energy that people gave me, I'm amazed at the depth of the resource my friends represented. I think the fact that help came so naturally is a testimony to its power. Maybe it's only at moments when your life is out of whack or falling apart that you get to see what a remarkable resource you have. When your life is normal that resource is hidden from your perception."

There was another type of support that Nikolas relied on during some particularly trying months. Despite his best-laid plans, the Gerbilator, the custom kiln, and the all the expert advice he could beg, there was an extended period when the project looked doomed. Time after time he would carefully stack the tubes as per the Gerbilator and fire up the enormous kiln to melt a panel into shape. But as the piece cooled, there would be a pop or a snap, and a sliver of a crack – often just a couple of inches long – would appear. When friends came by to drop off food and news of the outside world, Nikolas found himself confiding in them his darkest fears that he would fail.

"Friends represented a place I could go during those bad months to express the pain of the project – the depth to which I felt I was behind the eight ball," Nikolas says. "I experienced my friends as a repository for the tumors one accumulates during these experiences. When I could bitch and moan to friends about the lack of sleep and the anxiety, I always felt a bit lighter afterward. I could leave those thoughts behind and get back to work."

It's impossible to say whether Nikolas could have completed the job without the help and support of his friends. It's also impossible to know whether he would have been in the position to pursue this project had he had a wife and children. If he had attempted this Herculean task while trying to care for a family (or even a girlfriend), either the project or the relationships would have suffered. In the end, being single and surrounded by a loose community of friends proved a uniquely good environment for taking on such a gamble. While he didn't have much time to maintain his friendships, this didn't seem to damage them in the least.

"I could occasionally show up at parties," Nikolas said. "I was usually a zombie but appreciated that there was a bunch of people I could be around who wouldn't expect me to say anything. Just zoning out and absorbing the general feel of the group was comforting. When I couldn't go to a gathering, it was reassuring to think that my social world still existed and would still be there when I was done."

There was a subtler dynamic in play as well. Despite all the help his friends provided, on one level Nik was truly on his own. As empathetic as we were to the risk he was taking, it was not our risk. To Nikolas's thinking, this was a necessary part of the process.

"I think that moving ahead sometimes means leaving the group for a time and then returning with that new experience," he said. "When you experience something new you sometimes have to protect it from your friends on some level in order to assure that you won't be forced to see it through the familiar prisms. Sometimes you need to leave for a while, but that is made easiest when you know that the group will still be there when you return."

I took this to mean that the best groups provided support for risk but didn't coopt or lessen the meaning of the risk in the process. Groups of friends could help out and create a social safety net for the person on the high wire, but the risk had to remain a singular experience; otherwise, it lost its power to change the individual.

The Rising Tide Raises All Boats

"The fact that many of my friends were so impressed with the scale and nature of the project helped to balance the pain," Nikolas said. It was true that we encouraged him with our wonder at the scale of what he was attempting to create. But he wasn't the only one we took time to support. We had a half-dozen writers in our group, and each magazine piece or book contract was greeted with fresh enthusiasm. One scriptwriter was not only selling his screenplays to studios but also seeing them green-lighted to be made into movies. One friend was opening a law practice while another was getting promoted. Looking back, there seemed to be a constant sense that something good was happening to someone in the group.

It is worth pointing out that there was remarkably little competitiveness or jealousy surrounding these individual achievements. This was true even when our aspirations were similar. In the middle nineties, two writer friends and I rented a flat so we could have a shared office to go to where we could remind each other to keep at it.

We jokingly dubbed the place "the Writers' Grotto." We quickly filled the three other spaces with aspiring writers. A few years later we moved to a larger space, where we had room for nine writers, and a couple of years after that we took a five-year lease on an small building in downtown San Francisco and filled it with twenty-one novelists, journalists, and filmmakers. Our willingness to support each other had grown a community. Writers are a notoriously jealous lot, but at the Grotto we discovered that being part of a group allowed us to be happy for each other's individual successes.

In general, those in my tribe were excellent cheerleaders for each other – and why not? The world we lived in seemed filled with opportunity, so no one was possessed with the sense that the success of one had an impact on the chances of achievement for another. There was also the feeling that creativity and success would spread from one to another within the group. Sometimes this was literally true. John's film and my magazine story about Nik's project were examples of how creativity in one member of a tribe could directly spark creativity in other members. But for the most part, the success of one member brought with it the sense that we were all bound for great things. Each achievement increased the sense of certainty that lightning would strike again, close by and soon.

There was another, less obvious reason for our excitement. If friendships were a reflection of the self, the success of any friend made those around him or her look better. With the success of individuals in my tribe I felt as if the world was confirming my assessment of my friends and, by extension, confirming the reflection of my own best self that I saw in them. This wasn't at the front of our minds. Looking good myself was not my stake in Nik's achievement, and it was not the reason for my support. But it was certainly in the mix somewhere.

Of course it wasn't all successes. There were setbacks, opportunities missed, and flat-out failures, along with opportunities that just never seemed to surface for some. Larry, who played his songs at group events, was considered by many of us to be the most talented among us. Despite our efforts, his singing career never seemed to leave the ground. We pooled our money to buy him a digital recorder. A budding music promoter in the group took him on pro bono. We hooked him up with every musician and club owner we knew through friends of friends. Yet, to our amazement, every month he failed to show up on the cover of *Rolling Stone*. (I'm only half-facetious here. The fact that he had few regular club gigs did not diminish our belief that he could become the singer-songwriter for our generation overnight.)*

Such lack of success didn't seem to discourage anyone, especially Larry. There was always a forum where he received nothing but rave reviews, and that was at the hootenannies and houseboat trips where Larry performed for the tribe. This is another way our tribe encouraged the dreams of its members. When the world failed to confirm our talents, we could still declare each other gifted within the confines of the group. The fact that one's status in the tribe had little to do with worldly success also provided solace for those who experienced out-and-out failures such as being fired or getting dumped by a girlfriend or boyfriend. We praised and celebrated each other's successes, but there was no sanction for failure. This is what Andrea meant when she said that the security she found in her group allowed her to take risks in other areas of her life. Nikolas certainly knew that his friends, including me, would hold his place in the group until he finished his trial by fire. If he had lost his gamble – lost his enormous investment and failed at his shot at the big leagues – he could have come back into his group of friends every bit as valued as he had been before.

Discovering the True Self That Should Have Stayed Hidden

This dynamic of "finding your true self" and taking risks was all well and good if you had talents and goals like Nikolas's or Larry's. What if there was some flaw in your personality that made you prone to

---

* A small sampling of Larry's songs (including "The World's Saddest Girlfriend in the World") can be heard at www.urbantribes.net.

taking a risk with your life that was truly and monumentally wrong-headed? Did life in the urban tribe encourage those risks as well?

When Duncan first contacted me to tell me about his life, he had just moved from Manhattan to Wilmington, North Carolina, and was living a little like a man on the run. In his late twenties, Duncan was a big man – six feet, three inches – blond and handsome, with large hands and a goofy smile. He confided that his size and booming voice made him appear more confident than he often felt.

His life in Wilmington was nothing like it had been just a few months ago with his tribe in Manhattan. But that was the whole point of having moved down there: to stop the momentum of that life, to endeavor to change pretty much everything. Although heterosexual, he had found a job bartending at a venerable gay nightclub. Being the odd man out every night was fine by him. He was at a point in his life when he desired to be at the edge of the party. He had rented a house near the beach and took long swims in the ocean alone. He spent afternoons writing about his life in New York in an attempt to figure out exactly how he had ended up at this juncture.

Duncan's tribe years dated back to his early twenties. During and after his stint in the Army, Duncan lived in a handful of European and American cities. His sister, younger than him by two years, would often follow him around. As a brother-and-sister team they were outgoing and managed to quickly attract small groups around them. Being on the move themselves, they mostly drew in other travelers – people who were staying in cities for six months or a year but were soon on their way somewhere new. Everyone knew these groups would be short-lived. While the friendships were sincere, the groups were utilitarian, like the floating bridges used by the Army Corps of Engineers that could be put up in a day and disappear overnight.

When he and his sister landed in New York, they discovered that a half-dozen people from those overseas groups were already living in the city. Naturally and with little conscious effort, the people from those old groups rejoined. In less than a year there were twenty-five people whom Duncan could count on seeing regularly. Duncan and his sister purchased an apartment to share, and suddenly they were in a place where their sense of the future stretched out beyond the next season.

While the group was more permanent than the ones they had cobbled together overseas, there was a high turnover rate. Many of their friends were still in the middle of their travels, and as exciting as New York could be, it was still a place many people moved through. In the beginning, the group often felt inconsistent. When a key player would move on, or the holidays would roll around and friends would go back home, or people would get busy at work, Duncan would wonder, "Where did the group go?" But then, the next day or the next week, an e-mail would go out and the group would be gathering together again, as if there had never been a pause. The group would look slightly different, but the energy would be back.

Although not as celebrated as the disco days of the middle seventies, the late nineties were high times in New York, and Duncan's tribe had a remarkable thirst for everything the city had to offer. With the economy booming, there seemed to be good-paying jobs for anyone who had a can-do, let's-work-late-and-get-it-done attitude. It was a gold-rush atmosphere – the feeling that your wildest ambitions were achievable if you were clever or lucky or worked hard. Duncan was the twelfth person hired at a software startup that had $30 million in venture capital to get up and running. "We were all overpaid and underqualified," he admitted, looking back. "The company grew to over one hundred people. We spent tons of money on stupid things. It was a gravy train and we soaked it for what it was worth while the train was still moving."

Like most everyone in tribes, Duncan had great admiration for his friends. There was Edna,* who had "great artistic talent" and was making a living as "one of the best head-shot photographers in Manhattan. She was the most loving, mothering woman in the world. Always there to help." There was Bill, who sold air-conditioning

* For this story, for reasons that will become clear, I've changed the names of some members of Duncan's tribe.

systems for high-rises but was "an artist at heart who painted and played the guitar." There were Steve, who was a young executive in a construction company, and Kyle, a handsome college athlete who had recently moved from Southern California.

In Duncan's eyes, his friends were all on the fast track to the top. They were the people everyone wanted to be around. Asked to describe the attributes of his New York group, he gushed: "They were positive thinkers, smart, outgoing, loyal, loved a good party, open-minded, and very accepting of others. It was live and let live to an extreme."

There would be times when they would meet at a bar and literally take the place over. Other patrons would comment on the cohesiveness of the tribe and ask what the occasion was for the party. But there didn't have to be a reason for these instant gatherings. For Duncan, at these times, it would feel like he had made the city into his personal playground, like he would always know everyone in the room. He was under the spell of the illusion particular to New York: that his circle was at the center of what was going on in the city.

While individually they worked hard in their careers, when they got together, Duncan's tribe was about having fun. They went in on weekend and summer shares on Fire Island and in the Hamptons. They bought memberships at health clubs. There was a good restaurant on every other block, and someone often had an expense account to plunder. They enjoyed the thriving club scene and the bars that stayed open until dawn. Techno music was the perfect soundtrack for their lives. Pulsing and beat-driven, it blended one track into the next so they could just keep dancing, never experiencing the letdown of the song ending.

Drugs were one of the indulgences Duncan's friends allowed themselves. They smoked marijuana and took some Ecstasy, but it was cocaine that really suited their lifestyle. "We were functional users and we kept our shit together," he said pointedly when the topic of cocaine use came up. Duncan and his friends didn't get arrested, never bought or ingested their drugs on street corners. They called their drug dealers "brokers."

Cocaine was a fantastic drug for any endeavor from sex to hitting the nightlife to jamming out a business plan. It could be taken anywhere. All you needed was a rolled-up bill or the casing of a ballpoint pen and a CD case or a glass counter. The pulse-quickening experience of the high allowed them the sensation of matching the pace of the city. The drug made them more gregarious, with each other and with people they met along the way. Everything the group did was made a little brighter and a lot more interesting. The conversations were more intense, and the dancing went later into the night. The euphoria brought with it the sense that Duncan was sharing special moments with his group. Steve and he started a book club in which they would get together once a week, snort cocaine, and have, as Duncan put it, "endlessly worthwhile conversations."

There was something else, too. For the men, the cocaine seemed to be a replacement for something that had gone missing in their lives. As younger men, they had seemed to have more outlets for a certain type of testosterone-fueled drive. Many of them had been athletes but after college no longer had the time or the forums to pursue their sports of choice. For a while there seemed to be enough interest in the race to get laid. But then enough of them got girlfriends that the thrill went out of that game as well. The tribe's nightlife became not just about having fun but a competition to see who could have the most fun for the longest time. "That's when the group started turning up the heat on what was until that point our occasional drug use," said a friend of Duncan's. "The measure of who was cool had everything to do with how you tackled your nightlife. In a snap cocaine became a staple of the nights we went out. No one was prepared for how difficult it would be in your late twenties to keep all your ducks in a row while partying." In the competition to have the most fun, cocaine was the preferred performance-enhancing drug.

Although he was only a weekend user in the beginning, Duncan found himself thinking about cocaine during the week and looking forward to the next party with his friends. "It's like any memory of love," he wrote in an essay about his drug use that he shared with me.

"The recollection of the intimacy is always greater than the intimacy itself . . . [You remember] only the sensation of that very first line of cocaine, the sudden surge of overpowering sexual energy."

In the early days of his tribe's group cocaine use, an outsider might not have even noticed the presence of the drug or have any awareness that it had already begun to pervade the thoughts of many in his group. As the use of the drug became common at group events, etiquette was established that allowed the consumption of the drug while maintaining the message that they had everything under control. This was important, especially for those like Duncan who worried privately about the intensity of their desire for the high.

This etiquette required, for instance, that you didn't express anything more than a casual interest in knowing when or with whom the cocaine would arrive at a party or how much was going to be available. It was considered creepy to seem anxious to get high. The same rules dictated that when the cocaine did arrive, you weren't to rush right over all excited. For Duncan, this sometimes took "heroic restraint." He knew he had to act cool, the way he might if a celebrity had come into the room. You tried not to look directly, while at the same time keeping the revered guest in the corner of your eye. You had to wait for a graceful opportunity to make the acquaintance.

The hosts of the party, along with the person who had arranged for the arrival of the coke, would usually have first access to the drug. They would quietly disappear to a bedroom as the party went on without them. Duncan always knew exactly what was happening with the stash but knew not to talk about it. If the subject of the cocaine came up in conversation at all, it was understood that you would exaggerate the amount of time since you last used the drug. You could even pretend that you didn't remember how long it had been. Your attitude was expected to be something along the lines of "Wow, someone brought some cocaine to the party? What a novelty!" Everyone around you was likely to know that you were lying. Some of them might even have been with you the weekend before. The truth was less important than the message the etiquette was intended to send: We have our drug use under control.

When you finally made your way into the bedroom or the den where the cocaine was being doled out, the etiquette required that you offer but not be overly eager to help pay. Hundred-dollar bills would be offered and pushed away. This hid another subtext everyone understood: People who were allowed to contribute would be entitled to consume more than everybody else. The issue of who paid would become especially important at the end of the evening as the supply became smaller and smaller. Nothing would ever be said, of course, but everybody knew that everybody else was keeping careful track.

The smallest missteps in this etiquette could have serious sanctions. If you were too eager or spent too much time in the bedroom ingesting more than your share, you became a liability to the group's belief that the use was nothing out of the ordinary.

Freedom to Take the Wrong Path

The strict etiquette managed to maintain for a time the lie that everyone's cocaine use was manageable. Were these friends reflecting each other's best selves? I mentioned above that friends didn't necessarily mirror your true self, but rather an idealized notion of who you were. In this case the idealized notion was that Duncan and others were just recreational users of cocaine and no one was going to become an addict. Everybody, including Duncan, wanted this to be true for themselves and their friends. That these friends wanted to see the best in each other was having a perverse effect: They were creating and maintaining a group delusion that allowed those prone to addictions to establish their craving.

I knew something of this dynamic from my life. In the middle nineties, a subset of my tribe had the guilty pleasure of liking to gamble. Carloads of us would sometimes head to Reno for the weekend to play blackjack. While several of my friends liked to gamble, I discovered I had a particularly intense interest. In the beginning, I had a remarkable string of successes that became part of the lore of my tribe. My friends all agreed that I was naturally lucky and told stories of nights when I played blackjack and couldn't seem to lose. They recognized my passion for the turn of the card and encouraged it.

A couple friends and I soon discovered that there were poker houses within a few miles' drive from San Francisco, where we could play Texas Hold 'Em against tables of Asian men. I loved everything about those casinos. I loved the fact that you could eat delicious Filipino dinners while playing cards. I loved the shadowless lighting and the mirrored half-spheres on the ceiling that hid the cameras. I loved the idea that there were people watching over me – people who had seen it all. I encouraged us to go often, and once there, I rarely wanted to leave. My friends started to drive separately from me because I was hard to drag away from the action.

When they asked later how I had fared at the tables, I would often lie, minimizing losses and exaggerating my wins. I liked the story that I was lucky. "Ethan doesn't have a gambling problem," Jen said upon hearing me tell the group that I had turned my second royal flush, "he has a night job." That I had turned two royal flushes in the course of a few months was either a sign that I was lucky (the odds of getting a royal flush are well over twenty-five thousand to one) or a sign that I was clearly playing poker far too often for my own good. Jennifer chose to put the positive spin on my behavior.

My friends weren't entirely laissez-faire about my new avocation. Richard, who was a psychologist, pointed out that my demeanor around a gambling table showed clear signs of addiction. I would get so focused on the game that I lost interest in friendly conversation. I didn't mind when my friends left early or when they began to demur from coming along with me. They were an unneeded distraction. To avoid Richard's concern, I simply stopped telling him about my trips to the card room.

Let me be clear that I am in no way blaming my friends for my intense interest in gambling. The point is rather that friends are good at encouraging our risk taking but generally not as good at weighing in on the dangers or merits of those risks. Freedom to take risks requires an acceptance of possible negative outcomes – the understanding that not all bets we make are sure things.

Should my tribe have organized to address my problem? At the height of my interest in poker, I'm not sure what an intervention would have accomplished. I might have simply pushed them all away. The fact that they mostly maintained (against the evidence) that I had a passionate interest and not an addiction had an interesting effect. It felt as if they were holding onto the conception of my best self while I took a vacation from it. When I eventually pulled myself out of the spin toward addiction, I simply stepped back into the person they maintained had never left.

The Slow Split

Over time, Duncan began to perceive a split in the group between those who obsessed over the drug and those who didn't. The split could sometimes be seen at the same party: In one room there would be the usual socializing and in the other room there would be the outwardly friendly yet inwardly predatory focus on the doling out of the cocaine.

Soon, a few people stopped using the drug and felt uncomfortable when it was around. When the cocaine arrived at parties, these folks would slip away, saying they had had a bad week and needed to get some sleep. Everyone knew why they were leaving, and there was an inescapable pang of shame for those who eagerly stayed. That brief feeling of shame was easier, of course, than having a nonuser stick around. "No one using cocaine wants to be around someone who doesn't partake," said Duncan. Those friends who began to abstain were a dark mirror to Duncan's actions, and they were showing him something he preferred not to see.

Eventually the group's events fell into two categories, ones in which cocaine use would be a main attraction and others in which it was expected to stay hidden or downplayed. Duncan could predict, depending on who was holding an event, the presence and prominence of the drug. At some gatherings, the drug could be shared only among two or three people in the privacy of locked bathrooms. At other gatherings, cocaine would be displayed on glass-top coffee tables in the middle of the party.

There were no firm distinctions between these two factions and no overt judgments about behavior. They were "live and let live to the extreme." Duncan's tribe had formed organically and it began to split in just such a manner. At the parties where there would be a lot of coke, certain people were less likely to show up. At gatherings where the use of the drug was tacitly discouraged, the enthusiastic users were less likely to attend.

"Among a part of the group the drug became ubiquitous," Duncan said. "There were people who didn't go anywhere without doing it."

Duncan doesn't believe that the segment of the group that became regular users of cocaine ever really coalesced into a tribe of its own. Having cocaine as their common interest was a compelling reason to get together but made for an illusory emotional bond. All the things that unified the group in its beginnings – the mutual interests, the avocations, even the sexual flirtations – took a backseat. Even their conversations became increasingly ridiculous. "When we were doing cocaine, we didn't care what we were talking about," said Duncan. "It was no longer the conversations or even our friendships that were keeping us together."

The subgroup in Duncan's life that existed largely out of a devotion to the drug reached its own toxicity level. Like a virus that kills its host, the subgroup's interest in cocaine began to pull them apart. Money became an issue for some of these participants. Cocaine was expensive, and many were no longer as free with the hundred-dollar bills. The greediness that at first had to be hidden came to the surface. "Sometimes, at the end of the night, there were rumors that coca was still at the party, tucked away in some room to be shared by a privileged few," remembered Duncan. The etiquette intended to communicate that everything was under control became harder to maintain. A budding addict himself, Duncan didn't like being around others who appeared to lack control over the substance. That was another mirror too distressing to look into.

Addictions formed in a group don't die when the group falls apart. At some point, Duncan no longer needed the excuse of a party to get high. He had passed the need to lie about the last time he had snorted coke. With little effort Duncan obtained the phone numbers by which the drug would be delivered straight to his door. There was no French Connection intrigue. It was easier than ordering a delivery of Peking duck. Duncan found himself often looking in his checkbook and calculating whether he could pay his bills if he made another call to his "broker."

Once he began buying the substance for himself, he started to look for sexual and social companionship away from his tribe in the anonymity that was New York's other lure. His tribe of friends, composed mostly of the people who had their drug use under control, still existed, and he knew he was welcome there. But cocaine was his true passion.

In 1999 the gravy train at work began to slow down. As quickly as Duncan's company had hired its staff, it began to cut back. Soon there was news that the New York office of the company would be closed. He was faced with the choice of moving to Silicon Valley or being laid off. He chose to stay in New York. For the next year he lived on his severance and a small unemployment check. He biked across New England, then came back to Manhattan to hang out and do cocaine. He spent some time substitute-teaching in inner-city high schools and had short stints as a marketing consultant. Cocaine was the only constant in his life.

It was in New York that he hit the moment when he knew he had to change everything. His cocaine use had led to a series of unsafe sexual encounters, and he found himself one day sitting in a doctor's office waiting for the results of an HIV test. "In that waiting room, time, for all practical purposes, ceased," he remembered. "There was nothing behind me and nothing in front of me – just the results of the test. I saw both my dying and my living. My dying, a tragedy yet somehow fitting for my life, and my living, strangely, not a comfort – just one more opportunity to wind up in the doctor's office again, waiting on another HIV test. When the test came back negative, I decided neither way worked for me, so I moved."

Exile and a Phone Call

He was already in Wilmington, in his thirteenth week of self-imposed exile, when he got the call. "I have bad news," the friend from New York said. His friend Kyle had been found dead after a night of partying. Duncan had idolized the guy. Kyle was a remarkable figure of a man with a sense of personal confidence that made Duncan believe he would be a success in any endeavor. Talking with some other friends, he tried to piece together some of the story of what happened the night Kyle died, but the details didn't mean much. He already knew the story. He had lived the story so many times – just without that ending. There was a party and, of course, cocaine was there. Kyle had likely taken too much and his heart had stopped.

Duncan didn't go to the funeral. He didn't like funerals, but he also knew there would be cocaine, and he was trying to keep himself out of harm's way. Sure enough, as Duncan heard later, some of Kyle's friends stayed up all night grieving and reminiscing over lines of the drug. They rationalized that Kyle would have wanted it that way.

In the part of Duncan's group that didn't lose itself to cocaine, there remained no strict moratorium on the use of the drug, and every now and then there was a wild night out. But cocaine was not their focus. Recently, they got together on Thanksgiving and called Duncan to say how much they missed him. Duncan said that he knows a place remains for him there – among a group of people who believe that he can overcome his addiction. That Duncan's group was complicit in his cocaine use doesn't mean that it was to blame. Tribes provide us a remarkable forum in which to take personal risks with our lives, but we choose which risks to take on our own.

At their best, urban tribes can be counted on to maintain hope in the individual when we choose risks that lead us toward the edge of an abyss. Our tribes can remind us of our best selves at moments when we have forgotten what that best self looks like. An addiction or a failure or a romantic breakup might leave us with low opinions of ourselves and pondering any number of self-destructive actions. Our friends, at such a juncture, can challenge our self-loathing and forestall our bad acts by saying something along the lines of "This way you are feeling now, this way you are considering acting – *this is not who you are*."

Chapter 4

HOW TRIBES CONNECT A CITY

In the middle 1990s, when a sociologist named Robert Putnam first began publishing statistical papers showing recent generations had diminishing amounts of community spirit, I, along with almost everyone else, believed his premise. A few years later, when his work was cobbled together in a book titled *Bowling Alone*, he had gathered together a seemingly undeniable mountain of evidence describing the loss of what he called "social capital." "By virtually every conceivable measure, social capital has eroded steadily and sometimes dramatically over the past two generations . . . The quantitative evidence," Putnam concluded, was just "overwhelming." Besides not joining bowling leagues, my generation was not finding community among our neighbors, not going to church socials, and not joining our parents' civic or political organizations. The numbers proved that we had collectively turned away from the responsibilities of community building in the way a mule-headed teenager avoids yard work to sit alone and play video games.

Almost every statistic he found showed that my generation of young adults was less trusting of government, more prone to "malaise" (headaches, indigestion, sleeplessness), and even less likely to send greeting cards. Our grandparents, as a counterpoint, belonged to almost twice as many civic associations as we did. They were also more than twice as likely to trust other people (50 percent versus 20 percent).

In my favorite section of Putnam's book, he lines up forty graphs, eight per page, to show the decline in the various organizations that he gathered statistics on. Several of the lines showing the membership for these groups look like mountains, with their memberships peaking in the middle 1940s and 1950s, then slumping down. Some organizations show a more EKG heartbeat pattern, spiking and cratering several times over the course of the century. Nearly all, however, show a dramatic black-diamond slope downward between 1980 and 2000. This is, no doubt, why Putnam displayed them this way. The decline in organizations as diverse as the Jaycees, the Business and Professional Women, and the League of Women Voters appears remarkably consistent.

As these graphs suggest, Putnam looked for evidence to back up his gloomy conclusion in organizations such as bowling leagues, Rotary Clubs, and church social groups. Initially, I wanted to deflect his belief that we were less civic minded by dismissing the decline in these groups as a matter of fashion. The idea of going to a Shriners meeting and listening to some high school student read her award-winning essay on the value of democracy seemed like an activity that I might encounter in the first ring of hell. But to think that I would avoid such civic organizations because I was too hip to wear a fez unironically was, on examination, a shallow reason. It seemed to be only a further expression of the very problem Putnam was pointing out.

The consequences of our diminishing social capital are grave indeed, according to Putnam. "People who are socially disconnected are between two and five times more likely to die from all causes," he warns. Not only were our communities and our democracy at risk during this "anti-civic" contagion; apparently we were more likely to die young and alone.

So who or what does Putnam blame for this decline of social capital? Ever the statistician, Putnam serves up his answer in a neat pie chart. By his reckoning, the increased pressures on our time and money (as exemplified by the two-career family) are responsible for about 10 percent of the decline. He blames suburbanization for another 10 percent of the problem. Television and other forms of time-consuming electronic entertainment are 25 percent to blame. This left over half the blame on what he calls "generational change." It wasn't exactly clear to me how television and dual-income families could be separated from "generational change." In making the case that the specific variables could not account for this "generational change," it is as if Putnam wanted to show that we were born selfish – a generation of bad seeds.

"By any standard, these intergenerational differences are extraordinary," writes Putnam, adding that there is "little reason to expect that the youngest generation ever will come to match their grandparents' level of civic engagement."

In the end, all the pie charts, graphs, and statistics only prove what everyone, including myself at the time, already knew, or rather felt we knew. "Most Americans did not need to see charts and graphs to know that something bad was happening in their communities and in their country," Putnam writes revealingly. "Americans have had a growing sense at some visceral level of disintegrating social bonds." Putnam was just giving the evidence to back up our foregone conclusions.

Indeed, there did seem to be a general agreement that the excess of freedom that my generation enjoyed was leading to social disaster. Everyone, from Hillary Clinton ("It takes a village") to George Bush Senior ("a thousand points of light"), yearned for a revival of a community spirit that they believed was ebbing away. Of course, the political left and right differed on who and what was to blame. Liberals tended to argue that the global marketplace had undermined communities, as David Brooks observed in *Bobos in Paradise*, while conservatives maintained that the decline of community spirit was because of the breakdown of something they called "traditional morality." Both sides, however, seemed to agree that the lures of individual freedom were distracting us from the responsibilities of building community.

Although pretty much every politician and social pundit saw the decline of community spirit across the board, the yet-to-be-marrieds of my generation were often singled out for particular scorn. Given that we were unburdened by the responsibility of family, it was easy to portray us as overeducated, privileged no-goodniks uninterested in pitching in for the common good.

This seemed especially true in cities, where many had long assumed the very idea of community had broken down. Robert Ezra Park wrote in 1925 that although cities allowed many opportunities for an individual to have contact, urban living has made these "contacts and associations more transitory and less stable." "A very large part of these populations of great cities . . . live much as people do in some great hotel, meeting but not knowing one another," he wrote. "The effect of this is to substitute fortuitous and casual relationships for the more intimate and permanent association of the smaller community." Seventy-five years later, listen to the similarities as a Salon.com columnist laments city living: "There is a loneliness to American life today . . . In cities most public spaces are indistinct, impeccably designed by corporate creatives – the towering pillars of the Banana Republic at the outdoor mall, the endless escalators and tiled walls of the multiplex . . . Jobs come and go, people move away at the drop of a hat, relationships begin and end and begin again. It's understandable why so many of us long for some feeling of permanent connection."

A Different Style of Giving Back

It wasn't until my discovery of the widespread nature of urban tribes that I began to wonder whether we, as a generation, deserved a little less scorn and a little more credit. What if the community spirit of our grandparents' generation had been resurrected in a form we had yet to name? "Even if . . . Americans have withdrawn from public activities such as politics and civic clubs," writes the savvy Berkeley professor Claude Fischer, "the question arises as to whether they have withdrawn all the way into their isolated, lonely selves, or have withdrawn into a more private world of family, work and friends."

I knew the generosity expressed among bands of friends would not qualify any of us for a Nobel Prize in community building, but it seemed like it at least deserved an examination. I was not interested in making the case that this type of community building among friends was necessarily better than our mother's or grandmother's style. Initially, I just wanted to make the case that my generation was on the playing field.

But was giving in the context of friendships fundamentally different from giving in the context of one's larger community? According to Putnam, generosity to a friend should not be compared to generosity to a community at large. For the most part he belittles those who devote themselves to friendships, labeling them "schmoozers," as opposed to the upstanding "machers" who volunteer for the library board and the like. "The average American in recent decades has been far from isolated civically or socially," he writes, "but we seem engaged with one another as friends (or schmoozers) than as citizens (or machers)." What goes on between schmoozers, Putnam assumes, is inwardly focused "bonding," while what occurs in the civic organizations is outwardly focused "bridging." "Bridging social capital can generate broader identities and reciprocity, whereas bonding social capital bolsters our narrower selves," he writes. Putnam's general argument is that machers with their community involvement are the ones who really make a difference, while the schmoozers can still be infected with his "anti-civic" contagion.

Clearly there were meaningful differences between my tribe and the civic organizations my parents participated in. As a thirty-year member (and recently president) of her chapter of the League of Women Voters, my mother had helped organize dozens of nonpartisan candidate forums along with voter registration and education drives. When you talked about building community, these activities seemed like the ones to prize. Sure, my group of friends exchanged a few e-mails come election time, but as a group we seldom (read: never) organized ourselves to accomplish such civic good deeds.

But on another level, I wondered how clear a distinction there was between schmoozers and machers. First of all, I was far from convinced that everything that went on in a civic organization was "civic" in nature. Consider what goes on at a Lions Club meeting. Yes, they raise money for a local hospital or some such, but I imagined the baseline motivation for the membership was plain old schmoozing, with many members joining simply to get out of the house or, even more selfishly, to get a little more business down at the car dealership. I was willing to give them credit for an effective recycling drive that raised money for the children's wing of the hospital, as long as we put on the balance sheet every time an insider business deal went down between members. If my generation knew anything, we knew that those with the most impressive résumés in civic service could be the most Machiavellian and corrupt. I was also not willing to assume that everything that happened in these organizations built "bridges" to the rest of the community. With memberships based in the middle and upper middle classes, these organizations had a stake in the status quo. I had the suspicion that these organizations were composed of what insiders might refer to as "people like us." It may not have been written down who those people were, but you got the feeling that they knew them when they saw them. That the effect of these organizations might sometimes have been to keep the bridges down (between races or economic classes) was never explored by Putnam.

Whether maching was more important to civic groups than schmoozing remained an open question in my mind. I can tell you from personally witnessing many League of Women Voters meetings that the bond between these concerned women had as much to do with friendship as it had to do with promoting democracy. Although I didn't keep strict count over the course of my childhood, I would estimate that for every candidate forum the league sponsored over the years, there was at least one wine tasting.

While it was certainly true that not everything that happened at the Elks Club or the League of Women Voters was community spirited, it was beginning to become clear to me that not all that went on inside groups of friends was selfishly focused on our "narrower selves." My growing knowledge of urban tribes was waking me up to the fact that there was at least some maching going on among the schmoozers.

I went back to Putnam's book and searched it for any hint that he had seen a form of community spirit rising among groups of friends. I found this: "Twentieth century urbanization was not fatal to friendship," he conceded at one point. "Urban settings sustain not a single, tightly integrated community, but a mosaic of loosely coupled communities. As mobility, divorce, and smaller families have reduced the relative importance of kinship ties, especially among the more educated, friendship may actually have gained importance in the modern metropolis." It was an intriguing insight, to say the least, but unfortunately he didn't head in the direction it pointed. Putnam left his readers wondering what exactly went on within and among this "mosaic of loosely coupled communities." It was as if he had seen the urban tribe out of the corner of his eye but failed to turn and take a close look.

Follow Me on the Long Road to the High Ground

Although the evidence that I was part of an anticivic generation seemed, at first, unassailable, it didn't correspond with the way I felt. I did not belong to a bowling league or a civic organization. I wasn't part of Hillary's village or one of George's thousand points of light. Yet I felt extraordinarily connected to my city.

To understand what is happening in something as enormous as "American society," we must rely on numbers. But the fact that there are no numbers for something doesn't mean, necessarily, that that something doesn't exist. Having my own access to a thousand descriptions of urban tribes, I began to look through them, making a list of all the communal good deeds we engaged in through our groups of friends.

I did find a few tribes that directed their group energy out into the community. At holidays, some groups would throw parties to collect toys for the underprivileged, for example. Other tribes sponsored friends in charity races. One group in Cincinnati even organized free car washes, gave out cold drinks at intersections on hot days, and (I kid you not) voluntarily cleaned the public rest rooms of local businesses. Unfortunately, these groups – particularly those wacky Samaritans in Cincinnati – were the exceptions. The overt good deeds urban tribes accomplished were mostly for the benefit of the people in the group. As much as I would have liked to, I wasn't going to be able to make the case that urban tribes directly sponsored community-oriented projects. But despite the lack of concrete data, I couldn't shake the idea that these urban tribes somehow helped created community, and not just for their members, but for cities at large. My sense of belonging in San Francisco went beyond feeling accepted by my own group of friends.

While I was mulling over how this could be, a friend mentioned to me that I might look into network theory. I'm sure I should have been embarrassed that I had never heard of network theory. (Having attended a state university, I seemed forever behind the times when it came to cutting-edge theories of any sort. Not only had I managed to avoid mention of network theory, I had also somehow navigated an English degree in the late 1980s without ever hearing the word "deconstruction" – at least, not that I can remember.) Nevertheless, with the help of the Internet and a trip to the bookstore, I began a crash course in theories of social network.

Within my first day of study, I saw a mistake I had been making. I had assumed that urban tribes were discrete entities that could be isolated and dissected into their component pieces. According to network theorists, this let's-take-it-apart-and-see-how-it-works ap-proach defined modern science over the last century. To understand the properties of, say, water, one had to understand how its molecules worked, which required that you had to understand the properties of atoms with their electrons, neutrons, and, for all I know, ions and protons. This approach was useful, no doubt, but the pieces always needed to be broken down further, and by the time you were looking at the subatomic level of something, you were frustratingly far away from the thing itself.

In trying to figure out what urban tribes were, I had been attempting to isolate them – to count their members, categorize their roles, and define their borders in time and space. I was trying to make them distinct and separate from the social world of the cities in which they existed. According to network theory, this was a mistake. The meaning of these groups lay not in how they were separate from the social landscape of the city, but rather in how they were connected.

How a Social Network Theorist Examines Your Life

A network theorist might begin to examine your tribe by asking you the following questions:

1. Who are the people you'd call to discuss a romantic heartbreak?
2. Who are the friends you could ask to borrow money?
3. Who are the people you'd ask if you needed someone to stay at your house?
4. Who are those you would talk to if you needed advice about a problem at work?
5. Who are those you could call to take you out and cheer you up?
6. Who are those you'd call if you were moving or painting a room and needed a hand?
7. Whom would your friends invite if they were throwing you a surprise birthday party?
8. Who are the people you'd share a sport or an avocation with?

The names that came out of these questions would compose the key players in what University of Toronto researchers would call your "personal community," that is, a "social network defined from the standpoints of the Egos [a.k.a.: you] at its center." No one pays any membership dues to belong to your personal community, and you don't give out membership cards – you simply perceive it to exist.

This list in hand, the social network theorist could draw a sociogram of your social network. She would start with a dot (or node) indicating you, at the center, then draw lines radiating out to other dots indicating the friends whose names came up in the first five questions. Obviously the first five questions would elicit smaller numbers of people than the latter questions because they indicate a stronger connection and deeper trust. Most people average about three close friends or kin in these categories. The number of times the same person appears on the list is a rough indication of the strength of the social gravity he or she exerts on you.

Her next steps in drawing your sociogram would be to include the names that begin to appear at question number six. She could draw slightly longer lines to connect your dot to these names, indicating that they exert slightly less interpersonal gravity on your life. These might be the people you see when larger groups of your friends gather. Indeed, you may know them only within the context of these groups and spend little time with them one-on-one. Your sociogram at this point may look a little like a picture of an exploding firework with you at the center.

The sociogram your friendly social network theorist has created so far would describe your group of friends from your perspective, but in all likelihood it would not describe the true nature of your group. To do so you'd have to pay the theorist overtime to build a similar sociogram from the perspective of each member of your personal community and then interlock them. She'd have to get creative with her graph techniques, because she'd have to figure out a way to indicate those relationships that are asymmetrical in nature – those cases in which someone thinks he is a close friend to someone who thinks of him only as a casual friend. What you'd have when she completed this diagram would look something like a picture of fire-works finale, when all the rockets explode at the same time.

The resulting sociogram of your urban tribe would likely interest a network theorist for a couple of reasons. If your tribe were anything like mine, the heart of your sociogram would be a dense mass of crisscrossing lines. As I discovered early on, those within tribes tended to know almost everyone else. This would likely surprise those

Toronto researchers who believed that personal communities were usually "sparsely knit and loosely bounded," meaning that the people connected to the ego (node/you) at the center didn't necessarily know each other, and the ones who did know each other probably weren't that close.

All of these inwardly pointed lines would seem to argue against the notion that tribes are connected to their surrounding community, much less that they help bind those communities together. But if you looked at the edges of the sociogram, you would notice that not all the lines on the diagram pointed inward toward each other. Although your friends may share many or most friends in common, all of them will have relationships that exist outside of your shared group. If you wanted a comprehensive sociogram of all the people all your friends knew, you had better be ready to hire a phalanx of graduate students, because the graph would soon get widely complicated. If you included all the social ties of everyone you knew and everyone they knew and followed this out six steps, your sociogram would be quite large, because it would include every name of every person on the planet. This is the famous six degrees of separation.

That we are no more than six degrees of separation from anyone in the world is an interesting concept, but the social ties that actually affect our day-to-day lives are those within one or two steps of separation: that is, the acquaintances of your friends who exist just outside your shared group. In fact, if a social network theorist were to count the friends-of-friends network for the average member of an urban tribe, she would likely be impressed with the total number of what she would call "weak ties." Tribes tend to maximize the number of these weak ties for two reasons. First, tribes increase the number of friends you maintain in your life. The more friends, the more acquaintances and friends of theirs you are connected to. In addition, because tribes are most common among a particular demographic (college-educated yet-to-be-marrieds living in cities), it would be likely that those friends of friends exist in their own tribes. When tribes connect to tribes in this way, you've hit the weak-tie jackpot.

Why would it be important how many of these weak ties you had? Mark Granovetter answers that question in one of the most widely cited sociological papers of our time. He suggests that the number of weak ties in one's social network is critical to one's success in such endeavors as landing a job or finding a place to live. Cities are complex places where access to information can mean the difference between realizing your potential and just getting by.

While one's closest friends will give you all the information they have – say, when you are looking for a job – this information is limited both by their relatively small numbers and by the likelihood that their information is redundant, owing to the probability they've learned the information from each other. It's the weak ties that are critical in such situations. According to Granovetter, the most successful job seekers are those who have access to large numbers of friends and acquaintances who themselves have a large numbers of friends and acquaintances.

Until the need comes up, "the strength of weak ties," as Granovetter calls it, is largely hidden from us. If you got arrested one night and called a friend for help, he might connect you with a friend or acquaintance of his who happens to be a defense lawyer. Just because you had never met or talked with this lawyer before doesn't mean that he was outside your personal network.

Here's another example, which is painful for me to recall. At Christmas several years ago my father suffered a stroke. That night, my brother, my mother, and I were in desperate need of advice to understand his condition and sort out our treatment options. I called a doctor friend who immediately connected me to a neurologist he had gone to school with. There I was, at midnight, in a small-town hospital, talking to the head of a neurology unit who lived in a city I had never visited. Before that moment, I had not heard of this neurologist. Was he part of my social network? A network theorist would say absolutely. The help he gave me that night represented strength hidden in my network of weak ties.

The permutations of our friendships and acquaintances and the connections available through our weak ties can be mind-boggling. One might legitimately ask why that social structure need be so complex. In the tribes humans lived in during our prehistory, the permutations of the relationships necessarily maxed out at a few hundred. No doubt this was emotionally rich and complex, but it was not mathematically complex in the manner our extended social networks are today. I came to believe that the large number of weak ties my friends and I had access to were not a byproduct of our urban settings; rather, it was the urban settings that created the need for that multitude of weak ties. Finding a job can be a ridiculously difficult task if you are just off the bus from college. Indeed, when we are just entering city life, every task can seem hard, from finding a good and safe place to live, to getting a good deal on a car, to learning where the interesting nightspots are. As I thought about the weak ties in my life, it became clear that my ability to navigate city life rested in large part on this shadowy social structure that existed one step removed from my ability to see it directly. As Granovetter put it: "The personal experience of individuals is closely bound up with larger-scale aspects of social structure, well beyond the purview or control of particular individuals."

My tribe provided me with two seemingly contradictory benefits simultaneously. It offered me emotional shelter by giving me a half dozen strong ties clustered together, while at the same time connecting me to the city with hundreds (possibly thousands) of weak ties that ran from friend to friend and tribe to tribe.

Nearing the End of the Long Road to the High Ground

While Granovetter showed that weak ties were valuable to the individual trying to navigate his or her way through the city, they seemed at first to have little to do with community building. But it was worth wondering: If our tribes were maximizing our weak ties within a city, might we be creating the social-science equivalent of dark matter – a force that was invisible but was nonetheless critical to holding everything together? Could these imperceptible weak ties add up to something important in the social structure of a city?

In theorizing that dark matter exists, cosmologists and astronomers don't try to measure it directly. Rather, they look to the movement of stars and the behavior of galaxies. That is to say, they work backward from the behavior of all the matter they can see to infer the existence of forces they cannot see. I wondered if the social dark matter created by weak ties could be similarly inferred.

In the early 1990s, researchers Karl-Dieter Opp and Christiane Gern at the University of Hamburg attempted to understand the social dynamics that led to the protests that eventually toppled the Berlin Wall. What compelled individuals to participate in such massive protests was an interesting mystery, because the East German government, at the time, had a habit of discouraging citizens (often with the use of guns and the threat of prison camps) from joining political organizations that might advocate German unity. If there wasn't a large organized apparatus to push the protest forward – if there weren't groups that could alert their members – how did so many hundreds of thousands know when and where to show up? And more important, *why* did they show up if the risk to each individual was so steep?

Surveying thirteen hundred East Germans about their individual involvement, the researchers concluded: "Incentives to participate were concentrated in personal networks of friends . . . Personal networks were the most important contexts for mobilizing citizens." They added that mobilization was most effective when these social "networks overlapped, i.e., when weak ties existed between networks" of friends.

Weak ties connecting groups of friends could, it seemed, have a social impact beyond the members of a given group. Apparently, this force held the power to change the course of history. Of course the dynamic of the protests in the former East Germany might have been the specific result of political repression at the time. Perhaps weak ties between groups of friends only became politically powerful when people were barred from joining traditional hierarchical organizations and groups. Was my cohort of city dwellers making any use of the strength imbedded in the millions of weak ties that existed between us?

The answer became apparent when I walked out of my office one Friday in 1998 and discovered an enormous swarm of bicyclists (over five thousand by one estimate) riding up Market Street in San Francisco. It was my first encounter with what people had dubbed Critical Mass. The next day, e-mails from a friend who had taken part clued me in on what I had witnessed. According to him, it was a protest organized through word of mouth, and he had heard that it was going to be a repeated on the last Friday of each month and would go on indefinitely.

But what did the event mean? What were they protesting? As my friend understood it, most people in Critical Mass were demonstrating to make the general point that people should reconsider their dependence on cars, that the city should allocate more resources to establish bike lanes, and so forth. Beyond those general points, however, what the protest meant was up for grabs. I learned later that other participants thought that Critical Mass was something of a populist uprising that was to do battle with everything from the spread of SUVs to corporate greed and free trade. These more radical participants were the ones often featured on the television news reports expressing their pride that Critical Mass had shut down city traffic, using their numbers to "cork" intersections. Still other riders didn't seem to care much about the political meaning of the event, reporting instead that it was simply "the best party in town." The event seemed to allow each participant to make up his or her own story. On a video clip I saw of the event, the participants themselves expressed this confusion over what Critical Mass meant. In the clip, a few hundred bicycles were blocking the entrance to the Stockton Street Tunnel, chanting, "We need a slogan!"

"It was the embodiment of grassroots decision making, fraught with splits and cross-purposes, as well as reconciliation and community problem solving," one participant wrote in an e-mail that was forwarded to me by a friend. In telling his or her story of the protest, each member got a chance to personalize the experience: to squeeze out from the event the meaning he or she chose. As the e-mail concluded: "Because no one is in charge on our monthly ride and no specific ideology is set forth, participants are free to invent their own reasons for being there."

The range of opinions and tactics among the riders proved frustrating for those poor city bureaucrats who wanted to negotiate with someone who represented the mob so they could appease the protesters' demands or at least set out an official route for the thousands of bicyclists to take. But there were no leaders or spokes-people – when the next last-Friday-of-the-month came, even the mob itself refused to stay unified. When Critical Mass hit some internal critical mass of its own, groups of participants would split off into smaller groups, referred to as "mini-masses" or "minis." After the fifth-year anniversary of the start of the monthly protests, one participant described the action: "There were at least a dozen mini-masses crisscrossing their way around the city. We would split up here and there and other minis would join up when they met. It was particularly fun at intersections where the cross traffic was another mini. Folks would ask where the mini was going and join up if they liked the sound of it."

Regardless of what you might think of its methods or various possible meanings, it was impossible to deny that Critical Mass was a significant community happening that had a life of its own. Within a few years, Critical Mass demonstrations had spread around the world. Over seventy cities worldwide held Critical Mass rallies. Over the years it has been in existence, hundreds of thousands of people have participated in these rides.

Critical Mass became a case study of what came to be called "all-channel network protest." Like the protests in former East Germany, participants didn't take instructions from any leader or organization. Rather, they communicated primarily with other participants through personal networks. Large all-channel events or protests relied on two critical aspects: (1) knowledge of the happening, spread through the weak ties that existed between groups, and (2) motivation to participate, through the strong ties – that is, friends influencing friends.

As best I could discern, the force behind the creation and the eventual spread of Critical Mass to other cities was exactly the same force those German researchers had identified as critical to the protests that brought down the Iron Curtain. The strength of the weak ties between personal networks was responsible for the quick communication of information.

The key difference was that with Critical Mass information could be spread much more quickly through a pre-existing network of group e-mails. Through gossiping and planning private events, tribes were already adept at sharing information from one personal computer to dozens of others in the blink of an eye. The news of a protest or larger community event simply coopted this network, traveling the exact same routes we used to share all the other news of our lives. The process couldn't be easier. One tribe member could e-mail everyone else in his or her group, and if that information was particularly interesting, it could jump to other groups through the weak ties that connected one tribe with other tribes. By sending information to our friends, we could inadvertently spread information across a city, and even around the world.

Knowledge of events like Critical Mass was easy to share, but the motivation to actually show up usually required the individual encouragement of someone we knew well. "Personal friendship and bonding experiences may lie behind the successful formation and functioning" of personal networks, wrote two RAND researchers, John Arquilla and David Ronfeldt, in their seminal work *Networks and Netwars*. "The full functioning of a network . . . depends on how well, and in what ways, the members are personally known and connected to each other . . . Strong personal ties, often ones that rest on friendship and bonding experiences, ensure a high degree of trust and loyalty."

I never rode in a Critical Mass event, but I was not out of the loop. Several of the people in my urban tribe were regulars. I kept up with their exploits through the e-mails they would send the group before-hand, inviting everyone to join in, and afterward, describing what had taken place. I imagine my tribe's communication in this manner was quite common: A few members passed on information they heard from others (weak ties) and encouraged us to participate through peer pressure (strong ties). This pressure wasn't overt. No one ever said the equivalent of "Do this or I won't respect you," or "Our tribe has agreed to do this together." It was a milder form of peer pressure, more along the lines of "You should come with me, it might be interesting."

Of course Critical Mass didn't happen entirely spontaneously or organically. Someone had to have the idea, and some subset of people had to begin to put the word out. But because Critical Mass had no advertising budget, no official apparatus of decision makers, and no membership roles, it had to rely on firing up the connection of social networks, such as mine, that pre-existed within the city.

Much of the writing surrounding all-channel networks has been frightening treatises on terrorist organizations. It was obvious to me that leaderless bands of terrorists were a frightening threat, but it was equally obvious that this sort of network had many positive (or benign) uses. Critical Mass was not isolated in the least. The same networks of strong and weak ties powered Burning Man and the Rainbow Gatherings along with many radical environmental organi-zations such as Earth Action League. There were many more non-political uses of these networks, ranging from spring-break gatherings of college students at places like Palm Beach, Florida, to the rave dances, popular in major cities. No one was officially invited to a spring-break gathering or a rave – you simply heard about the event through weak ties and then, among your close friends, decided whether or not to attend.

I came to believe that these all-connection networks were most common on a scale significantly smaller than protests like Critical Mass. The sudden rise of "house concerts" was a good use of connected networks. By 2001, house concerts had become a valuable venue for solo musicians. House concerts relied on the strong ties of an individual tribe of friends. A performer was booked for a given night and e-mail was sent out. The hosts passed a hat at the end of the concert asking for ten or fifteen dollars per person. If the performer could sell some CDs, his or her take could run from $300 up to $1,000 performing for a group of just a few dozen in a packed living room.

While individual house concerts were promoted through highly clustered groups of friends, the fact that they existed as a national trend owed to the strength of the weak ties that connect like-minded sets of friends across towns and across the country. It was only through those networks that a group in one city could learn which performers were coming through town and when. Musicians who created good word of mouth through their performances could go from city to city almost indefinitely, following the network of weak ties that connected urban tribes.

While Putnam took a lot of time in his book to document the decline of organizations as small as the Charity League of Dallas and something called the Little Rock, Arkansas, Sertoma Club, which was down to only seven members for its weekly luncheons, he dropped the ball when it came understanding the social dark matter hidden in our weak ties. He makes no mention of Critical Mass or the rise of house concerts or the loose networks of pickup ultimate Frisbee played every day in cities across the nation.

While Putnam was right in that I had never joined a bowling league or a community service organization, he clearly didn't understand that through one or two degrees of separation I could tap into a massive network and put it to work. Through this network, I could have found dozens of activities to throw myself into, not just in San Francisco, but in any major city, on any given night. That activity might be as important as a meeting to plan a protest or as frivolous as a rave. Regardless, my network of weak ties made me feel uniquely connected to the swirl of city life in our modern times.

Like dark matter, it's hard to document these weak ties in action. With events such as Critical Mass, their power can be inferred only retrospectively. Without John Ashcroft on your side, tracing the pathways by which information spreads through group e-mails about Critical Mass would be impossible. However, every now and again something happened so that the strength in weak ties became slightly more visible.

One such example came along after an MIT graduate student named Johan Paretti read that Nike was offering the option of personalizing its shoes by stitching a name or phrase of the customer's choice. As a lark, Peretti ordered a pair of Nike shoes emblazoned with the word "sweatshop." When the company refused, Johan got into an e-mail exchange with some Nike functionary over the question of just exactly why Nike wouldn't put the word on its product (the back-and-forth can still be found at http://shey.net/niked.html). When it was over, he e-mailed the exchange to a dozen friends, some of whom forwarded it to friends of theirs. From there, the e-mail spread like a virus. Although nobody knows for sure, estimates of how many people got that e-mail ranged from five hundred thousand to seventeen million.

Eventually, major media around the world featured the story. At one point, in what must have felt like a surreal experience, Johan found himself on the *Today* show debating a Nike spokesperson. "I was astonished that something I decided to share with a few close friends could replicate literally millions of times," wrote Johan later.

The important thing to remember was the effort it took to launch such a remarkable meme: He sent one e-mail to his tribe of friends. The evidence for how this e-mail was subsequently spread around the world through similar communities of friends often came back to Johan when someone at the end of a chain decided to e-mail him directly. He noticed that at the top of his original e-mail there was often a tacked-on phrase such as "John, I thought you would appreciate this," or "Check this out, Sarah." "Even though the meme went to millions of people," Johan later concluded, "the personal quality of the communication remained intact. People got the message only if it was recommended by a personal acquaintance. Social networks were the only way that the Nike sweatshop message could spread."

In his analysis of how his e-mail traveled the world, Johan missed a key element. Yes, the e-mail spread between friends, but it could not have jumped the boundaries of individual social groups (and cities and countries) in such a wildfire manner had it not lit up the networks of weak ties that exist at the edges of groups of friends.

I knew personally of another example of this phenomenon. During the research for this book, I managed to tap into the power of these weak ties. I received over a thousand survey responses and e-mails, none of which I directly solicited. They came to me through the Internet after the small magazine article coining the phrase "urban tribe" had been e-mailed among groups across the country and around the world in the same manner that the Nike e-mail traveled. I knew from personal experience that Putnam and all the other doomsayers had to be wrong. That such a large number of people from around the country would come out of nowhere to help a stranger with his book did not speak of a generation disconnected and cut off.

Return to a Different Type of Community Building

If my generation compared ourselves within the whole scope of American history (rather than just with the vaunted World War II generation), we might conclude that our grandparents' generation's devotion to civil service was more the exception than the rule. Perhaps what we were seeing in my generation was a swing back toward a type of generosity associated with good old American individualism. I used to be wary of this term, "American individualism," because it had often been coopted by people as an excuse for the rankest selfishness.

What I discovered, however, was that such individualism spoke of a fine tradition of Americans devoting their time and resources privately to individuals and groups (such as one's neighbors, one's extended clan, one's coworkers, a group of friends, a family business or ranch, etc.).

Listen to how a school supervisor from 1916 defined "social capital" long before Putnam came along and made the term synonymous with joining civic groups. Social capital was composed of "those tangible substances [that] count for most in the daily lives of people: namely good will, fellowship, sympathy, and social intercourse among the individual and families who make up a social unit . . . If [an individual] comes into contact with his neighbor, and they with other neighbors, there will be an accumulation of social capital, which may immediately satisfy his social needs and which may mean a social potentiality sufficient to the substantial improvement of living conditions in the whole community."

Notice that this earlier definition does not make social capital contingent on signing up for a bowling league or marching in a parade. The implication here is that social capital comes from much more fluid and informal (yet potentially quite close and intricate) connections between people. Under this definition, social capital could as easily accrue among a tight group of friends yet still have an effect on the community at large. I don't mean to blur all distinctions (rave $\neq$ Critical Mass $\neq$ League of Women Voters $\neq$ urban tribes $\neq$ spring-break beer party). However, the true moral and emotional value inherent in these types of community activities required a look beyond their labels or categories.

In the end, I was even prepared to make the case that there were things to recommend the tribal style of community building that took place through groups of friends. For one, this form of community building did not happen discretely in one part of our lives. The fact that our volunteering could not have been easily quantified and put in a statistic (as in: volunteering = five hours Rotary Club parade cleanup) perhaps meant that we had integrated our good deeds seamlessly into our lives. We were helping out those around us not out of a sense of social responsibility but as the very expression of who we were. While other generations might have made time to "give back to the community," we gave reflexively and without distinction between community building and the other activities in our days. Even the phrase "social capital" (with its metaphor of money and investment) implied a type of dynamic my generation seemed to eschew. We didn't want to "spend" or "save" social capital. We had reverted to a type of "social barter" that came more naturally to us.

I could see some other advantages as well. Because my tribe depended on no official apparatus, it required constant personal attention from its members to remain in existence. While one could declare oneself a member in good standing of a civic organization if one paid dues and attended a meeting every other month, the personal community I perceived in my life could not have survived such neglect. Passive participation was not an option. Such social networks required that we constantly groom each other by sharing gossip and helping each other out.

That friendship would be our forum for giving and community building began to make more and more sense. Our lives were fluid, unstructured, and made up as we went along; friendship was the relationship that fit into that loose structure. I was not surprised when I learned that gay cultural philosophers had seen this utility of friendship long before I did. Gay populations had been living outside of families in large urban centers a full generation before heterosexual yet-to-be-marrieds joined them in such large numbers. Homosexuals had already addressed the problems my group was facing (living outside of families, traveling uncharted social paths), and they had come up with the same solution: create loose, flexible friendship networks that were connected through weak ties to other networks.

"Friendship is for those . . . whose comfort in themselves is sufficient for them to want merely to share rather than to lose their identity. And they enter into friendship as an act of radical choice. Friendship, in this sense, is the performance art of freedom," wrote

117

Andrew Sullivan of homosexual communities in his book *Love Undetectable: Reflections on Friendship, Sex and Survival*. "Homosexuals, by default as much as anything else, have managed to sustain a society of friendship that is, for the most part, unequalled by almost any other part of society."

But it was exactly this "society of friendship" that I was seeing in my group of heterosexual friends. Simply put, I came to believe that my group was engaged in an experiment in the meaning, boundaries, and nature of friendship very much parallel to the experiment that continued in gay communities. We were finding out if friendship was strong enough not only to sustain us emotionally but to bind larger communities as well. This experiment in friendship was what we were doing with our freedom.

PART TWO

LOVE IN THE TIME
OF NERVOUSNESS

Chapter 5

THE STIGMAS OF SINGLE LIFE

Having developed some sense that we were not wasting our time living outside families, I began to turn to the question of just exactly why we were staying single so long. Urban tribes explained what we were doing with this time, but they didn't explain why this marriage delay had begun. To find the answer, I started by looking at pop culture, wondering whether the changing cultural views about singleness might have influenced our avoidance of marriage. In the late nineties, for instance, I began to find more and more stories in the popular press about the positive side of being single. The *Chicago Tribune*, for instance, broke the news that "dining alone can be a comfortable experience," while the *St. Paul Pioneer Press* ran a story under the headline "Confirmed Bachelorettes Are Shaking Off the Stigma of Their Single Status." People were "living single and living it well," reported the *Ventura County Star*. "One: Not the Loneliest Number," announced an upbeat cover story in *USA Today*.

The text of these articles generally attempted to send the message that being single in open-minded America at the turn of the millennium was not abnormal. These stories invariably quoted singles and "relationship experts" to make the case that single lives were happy lives. "Right now, I'm extremely happy," said Gloria, a thirty-two-year-old quoted in a *San Antonio Express-News* story. "I'm doing flamenco dancing," Pamela Stone, author of *A Woman's Guide to Living Alone*, was quoted in the *St. Paul Pioneer Press* story as saying. "There are so many women who told me they loved to be able to get up when they wanted

121

and to stay up in the wee hours and knit or sew . . . One woman painted T-shirts till three in the morning as Christmas presents."

Such dubious testimonies to the joys of being single went on and on. In these articles single women and men talked about how great it was to have "space" in their lives, to be able to "snore and go where they want to," and how they took "comfort in self-awareness" and in caring for their "emotional needs." Singles talked of "staying busy" and about the "freedom and joy" of not having to consult with a partner or a child to make decisions. "I'm in control of what I spend," declared a single salesman from Scotts Valley, California. "Right now, I'm thinking of buying a BMW convertible."

Relationships "experts" cheered the singles on. "Write lists of all the advantages to being single," advised one expert, while another encouraged singles to take themselves to sporting events and to "give friends those little valentines such as the ones they pass out at elementary school." One story even suggested that groups of singles go out on the town and make fun of the couples they come across. But above all, the single experts warned, we should remember that not being in a committed relationship "does not mean that something is wrong with you."

For the most part, these articles did not make me feel any better. Their timing was the first thing that made me wary about what they were really communicating. They often appeared in papers around Thanksgiving, Christmas, or Valentine's Day. While the editors and writers would certainly defend this choice by saying that these were just the times when singles needed to be cheered by such upbeat stories, they likely had the opposite impact. It was at such times of the year that newspapers were filled to the brim with heartwarming stories about families, marriages, and lifelong love. Put in this context, the lone story about the newfound joys of singleness seemed like the offhand throwing of a bone. It also seemed to me that stories on being single at such couple- and family-oriented holidays might have a sneaky dual purpose. Intended for the insecure single, they probably played well to the happily marrieds, who could read the pieces and gleefully reflect on how lucky they were not to be single at such times.

There was something else about these articles that that belied their intent. Look again at the details that were used to describe single life. Single life was trumpeted because people could snore or stay up until three in the morning to paint T-shirts or spend the night on the town making fun of couples or blow their money on BMW convertibles. Was I supposed to be relieved by being grouped with people who needed to be encouraged to "stay busy" by writing lists of why they are not unhappy? I wasn't sure I wanted to hang out with these people, much less be identified as part of their demographic grouping.

Then there was the fact that the experts quoted in these pieces would come right out and say things like "there's nothing wrong" with being single and that we "need not be depressed," as if such directives would make anyone feel better. That sort of ham-fisted advice, combined with the rather pathetic descriptions of what single life was all about, was hardly a sign that the stigma had evaporated. While the writers of these pieces might have believed they were our champions – vanquishing an evil social stereotype – what they ended up creating were documents that precisely pinpointed the current state of the stigma of being single.

Meeting the Advocates for Singledom

To go beyond the newspaper stories and find out what was actually happening with the stigma of staying single, I planned a trip down to L.A. to spend an afternoon with Tom Coleman, the executive director of the American Association of Single People, at the northern extremes of the Los Angeles basin in scenic Glendale, California.

When I told people my plan, I received strangely strong reactions. Some assumed that the AASP was a joke or some sort of nonprofit grant-sucking boondoggle. Others speculated that it might be a matchmaking service for swingers. When I explained what I knew about the AASP, that it was a sincere lobbying effort on behalf of nonmarried America, nearly everyone wondered aloud why single people would need such advocacy.

My own preconceptions were not insignificant. What kind of

person, I wondered on the flight down, would join the American Association of Single People, much less work there? No matter what I found, I was determined to keep a straight face.

The building that houses the AASP in Glendale was telling. As you might imagine, the AASP did not own a shining office tower but rented a small suite of drab offices on the third floor of a building that twenty years ago might have looked nice enough to house an insurance agency. Coleman, bespectacled and fiftyish with a carefully trimmed mustache, led me to the conference table, where three volunteers for the organization were stuffing envelopes for its quarterly newsletter. He introduced me to an attractive young woman named Kat, a handsome ponytailed man named Michael, and a rather large, possibly toupeed fellow I'll call Cliff.

Given that they were engaged in a mailing to AASP's members, the obvious first question was: Just how many people belong to the AASP? Coleman told me that he had about fifteen hundred current members. Given that he often positioned himself to reporters and legislators as a spokesperson for the 82 *million* single people living in the country, I knew right away that his organization's membership was a tiny percentage of that larger group. (When I later tried to figure out just how close to zero that percentage was, the calculator on my Macintosh computer managed only an error message. I eventually figured out that if you threw a party for 54,666 single people, on average, one of your guests would be a member of the AASP.)

As Coleman was the main spokesperson for the organization, it did not take much coaxing on my part to get him to launch into his spiel about the need for singles' rights.

"We're fast becoming a nation of singles," Coleman said before I had asked the question. "The Ozzie-and-Harriet family is only about 10 percent of all families. Diversity is now the norm. Within a few years, the majority of households in the nation will be headed by unmarried adults." Coleman's smile told me that he was clearly happy about these facts.

What he was not happy with, however, was that single people everywhere were getting screwed by governments, corporations, and

124

landlords, all of whom often discriminated against the unmarried. Among the injustices he was fighting was the fact that unmarried workers could receive up to 25 percent less pay for the same work as their married counterparts. This was because married workers often got a smorgasbord of health and pension benefits for their spouses that the single worker had no access to or compensation for. Landlords often would refuse to rent to single-parent families or to unmarried room-mates or couples. Singles got screwed on their taxes too, according to Coleman. Singles paid the same employment taxes yet tended not to live as long as married people and therefore were less likely to collect the benefits. In addition, surviving spouses could receive benefits for years, while the option of sharing such death benefits was not available to singles, even if they had long-term partners.

"This leads us to the situation where single black men are sub-sidizing married white women," said Coleman, who, I quickly learned, liked to put these inequities in the brightest possible contrast. The logic here was that single black men, who die much younger than married white women, were paying into a social security system that they were statistically less likely to benefit from.

The list of inequities went on and on. Insurance rates, parental rights, passing on inheritances, the legal meaning of "dependents" and "family" – all favored the married over the unmarried. On top of that, the laws in thirteen states still referred to children of an unmarried woman as "bastards," while the legal language in the other thirty-seven called them "illegitimate."

Coleman's list of grievances was impressive. What I feared was going to be a touchy-feely organization fighting against cultural stigmas was actually a hard-core lobbying group fighting to change laws and the treatment of single workers, renters, and parents. As he went on, I found myself becoming a convert to the cause, which was a sign that Coleman was good at his job.

What was particularly infuriating to me was not just the blatant unfairness, but that much of this discrimination was so intentional and aboveboard. Many of these laws had been put in place specifically to

125

encourage marriage at the expense of those who stayed single. Politicians, in fact, had been stampeding each other to be more profamily than the next guy, and nobody had been held accountable for the unfairness that resulted. Get discriminated against because you're single? Go cry in your beer, say the politicians. Federal civil rights laws did not prohibit discrimination based on marital status. Us singles were being discriminated against *intentionally* and for easy political gain. I found myself getting incensed that the government of a free country would see fit to try and muscle its people into certain acceptable ways of living and loving.

"In theory we live in a country that protects freedom of choice in our personal lives," said Coleman, in what sounded like the end of a speech he had given before. "People should have the choice to live in the household structures that best suit them. My dream is that freedom of choice will be supported by lawmakers and by the courts and private businesses. This is not true today."

"What do we need to do?" I asked. Coleman told me that the list of changes was long indeed. Some were obvious: We had to start by making it illegal to discriminate against someone based on their marital status, make sure that single black men who die young are not supporting married white women, and remove "bastard" from all the state laws.

But those changes were just the beginning. Coleman told me he believed we must lobby the corporate community and insurance companies to make it possible for singles to have access to the same health care and pension benefits that married employees enjoy. Coleman also advocated that states have "domestic partnership registries" by which unmarried couples could legally declare themselves responsible for each other's welfare and thereby gain access to the health care, child custody, and survivor rights to which a spouse would be entitled. It was plainly unfair that the surviving partner in an unmarried couple couldn't, for instance, sue a drunk driver responsible for the death of his or her partner when a surviving spouse could.

All of which made sense to me. But how, I asked Coleman, were we going to get the political leverage to make those changes?

126

"The only way change will happen is when unmarried adults stand up for their rights, protest discrimination, and organize politically," he said, not indicating how hard that was going to be. "The cost of being single in America is high because we have not yet united to fight this injustice."

Although his job as executive director of the AASP required him to stay upbeat on this particular topic, rallying singles to the cause seemed problematic. There were reasons, after all, that the AASP had only fifteen hundred members out of a pool of 82 million potential constituents. Even though Coleman had, to my ear, a rock-solid case that we are being treated unfairly, most singles didn't appear interested in joining together for political battle. Why? Perhaps there was some embarrassment in joining a lobby for "singles," but I imagined it had more do with the fact that most singles didn't intend to be single long enough to make a federal case out of it.

Sure, if we were not currently dating anyone, we were probably willing to admit that we'd be single for the next six months – but that was about as far into the future as we wanted to lock ourselves in. We didn't want to rule out the possibility that on any given tomorrow, in the checkout line at the supermarket, we might accidentally crash our cart into the cart of Winona Ryder's body double, which would be the start of a tornado romance and hasty but happy marriage. We had all heard stories of seemingly hopeless singles finding love and getting married in a season, and such is the optimistic nature of the human heart that we all believed that it could happen to us, too. Humans seldom give up hope – especially at times when hope is all we have.

All of which made the ten-dollar fee for a year's membership in the AASP very pricey – not because we couldn't afford the ten spot but because the year's commitment to singleness was a full half-year longer than our secret best-case scenario.

Once Coleman got down from his soapbox, he was willing to admit that getting singles involved in the cause was a bit of a problem. He had been on lobbying trips to Washington, D.C., where congressmen and their staffs listening to his agenda had been openly skeptical about the political might of his organization. An aide for Representative Lloyd

Doggett (who has expressed sympathy for Coleman's concerns) voiced her doubts about the power of the AASP to a reporter. "Where do they get their grassroots support from?" the aide asked after meeting with Coleman. "Do single people write letters? Do they mobilize?"

You can see her point. It was unlikely that there would ever be a Million Singles March on the Capitol. To have an effective lobby, you had to have a group willing to identify themselves as a group. There may have been 82 million Americans who were officially single, but how many of them wanted to wear a T-shirt to that effect? Wasn't the word "single" itself a barrier to rallying the troops?

"There is so much confusion over the word 'single,'" Coleman admitted with a sigh. "Widowed women don't consider themselves single, for instance, and people often associate the word with 'swinging singles.'" For the AASP, the word is a legal definition: every adult who is not married has the legal status of "single." But unfortunately for Coleman, this is not how the rest of the world uses the term. Any man with a girlfriend, for instance, had best not publicly identify himself as "single."

Coleman's organization was connotatively estranged from the majority of that unmarried population who use the word "single" almost exclusively to describe someone on the hunt for love. Ask someone on the street to use the word and you'll likely hear phrases such as "you should meet my single friend" or "single white male seeks single white female."

"Yeah, the word has definitely been a problem," Coleman admitted. "There is a lot of negative reaction to the word."

I pointed out that it's unfortunate his association's name contains that very troubled word. "True, I sometimes wish we had gone with the 'American Association of Unmarried People' instead." But that gets into its own can of worms, as Coleman explained, because the vast majority of the people who are unmarried consider themselves "not married currently" or "not married yet."

No, the problem Coleman faced in getting people to jump on his bandwagon ran deeper than semantics. I was far from alone in not wanting my public or political identity to be "single person."

As Coleman described the difficulties of getting people to back his cause, I tried to assess the man in front of me. Clearly he wasn't just a hired gun. Unmarried himself, Coleman's anger at the unfairness he battled was palpable and personal. Which made me wonder this: Given that there were so few people interested in being members of the AASP (even at the cost of only ten bucks a year), what would lead someone to become the executive director of such an association? People do all sorts of crazy things in this life, but they seldom choose long-term activities that make then less desirable to potential mates.

Coleman clearly wasn't doomed to singleness because of his looks or personality. He displayed plenty of confidence, and while not handsome by the high standards of Los Angeles, he would be considered good looking in most other contexts. He groomed himself well and kept his mustache neatly trimmed . . . Wait a second, I thought – that mustache was *very* neatly trimmed. And just the fact that he had a mustache and was neither a fireman nor a gym teacher from the Midwest . . . It began to dawn on me that singleness might have a specific meaning for Coleman that it didn't for me. There was, after all, one population of adults out there who will likely never have the chance to get married.

I finally asked the obvious question: Why was he single?

"I'm legally single," said Coleman. "But Michael and I have been partners for more than twenty years." Coleman nodded to the striking man with the ponytail patiently stuffing envelopes at the end of the conference table. Michael gave me a wink and a smile.

Well, that explained why Coleman would have no problem taking the job for the long run. It was unlikely that the AASP would lose its executive director to the institution of marriage any time soon, for Coleman was legally barred from marrying the person he loved. While homosexuals had a long-term stake in ironing out the inequities between singles and the married, Coleman assured me that his organization was not a beard for the gay lobby. He estimated that no more than 20 percent of his membership was gay.

Given his personal situation, I asked, "Why not lobby for gay marriage?" Coleman said that for gays to spend their somewhat small amount of political capital pushing for gay marriage was a mistake. "I believe that if gay marriage was legally allowed tomorrow, a majority of gays would never marry. Because homosexuals have been barred from the institution, they've pursued a different lifestyle. It would still be seen as a heterosexual institution that was not friendly to gays."

With this comment, I began to wonder whether Coleman was not just prosingle but antimarriage to boot.

"Are you against the institution of marriage?" I asked.

"I'm not against marriage in principle, but given the way the institution is used these days, you have to wonder why people think it's the bedrock of society," said Coleman. "While ninety percent of people will get married at some point in their lives, they don't do so for a lifetime. Many will marry and then divorce, maybe remarry and then become single because of the death of their spouse. For most people, marriage comes and goes in phases."

I told him that he had convinced me that singles were unfairly discriminated against, but it would be much harder for me to give up the belief that marriage was fundamentally a good thing for society.

"You have to consider the possibility that with marriage there is no there there," he said, a tone of annoyance coming into his voice. "I mean, fully half the people who pledge 'till death do us part' are lying. What does it mean when people getting married for the fifth or sixth time pledge their lifelong devotion? If you can get married again and again and each time opt out of the obligation . . . the institution itself begins to look hollow."

"The history of marriage in our culture is not that pretty," he continued. "Many feminists associate it with certain attitudes about women, and it often trapped people in bad relationships. Atheists and agnostics have also suffered because of marriage's close ties to religion."

Coleman, of course, did not want to revitalize the institution of marriage or go back to the days when it meant you were stuck for life, like it or not. Rather, he wanted marriage to be seen for what it was – an imperfect institution that did not deserve its status as the be-all and end-all of human relationships. "It really bothers me that marriage is perceived as better than all other commitments," he said. It became clear that in Coleman's worldview, lessening the stigma of being single required that we knock the institution of marriage off its pedestal.

Coleman quoted me a favorite survey that asked Americans which of the following best described family: (a) people related by blood, (b) people who live together, and (c) people who love each other. He happily reported to me that 70 percent of those surveyed picked "people who love each other" as the best definition of family.

"I'm not saying marriage is meaningless," Coleman conceded. "What is good for society is when people make meaningful commitments to each other's well-being. But that sort of allegiance does not happen just in marriages. I see no reason why a married couple should get more respect than a cohabiting couple. Marriage does not have the market cornered on commitment."

On this point, Coleman's crusade seemed the loneliest. Perhaps he could begin to turn the tide on the open discrimination against single adults, but I doubted that he would have much of an impact changing our cultural belief in the power and importance of marriage. The very idea of marriage, after all, exists on two distinct levels. There is marriage in the form of its conflicted real-world application, and capital-M Marriage in the form of its idealized meaning. We've all seen marriages go badly, but even those brutalized in the bitterest splits often still believed that the ideal embodied in the notion of Marriage was worth striving for. Coleman might as well attack the idea of love. After all, most people who say "I'll love you forever" turn out to be lying. But that doesn't diminish our belief that love is possible.

My Work for the AASP

I had promised Coleman that if he gave me an interview that day, I would make up for his time by helping stuff envelopes for that quarter's newsletter. So, as the interview wound down, we both pulled our chairs up to the conference table and joined Michael,

131

Kat, and Cliff and started to work. My first job was attaching pregummed labels to the envelopes. As I peeled and pasted, I tried to imagine the lives behind the names and addresses. Was the woman in Phoenix a single mother or widowed after a thirty-year marriage? Was the man in Seattle heterosexual or homosexual? Was he divorced or in a committed relationship outside of marriage? What had drawn them to the AASP? As I pondered the names, it occurred to me that when it came to stigma, the microcategories of singleness seemed more important than the commonalities.

Those of us around the conference table that day spoke to the spectrum of lives lived by single people. I learned that Kat, who sat next to me, was a twenty-one-year-old lesbian student doing an internship for the AASP. She had her own stereotypes to fight, as did the overweight, heterosexual Cliff, who was rambling on and on about his former job as a traffic school instructor. Sure there were unfair laws that affected us all, but the cultural stigmas that followed each of us couldn't be more different. The problem that Coleman faced in rallying the single troops might have had as much to do with the massive differences in the single population as it did with people's dislike of being labeled single. Perhaps we were not gathering together as an effective lobby because we didn't feel like we were part of the same group.

Sure, all single people might care about getting screwed in our benefit packages at work, but individually we were probably more concerned about less global and more heterogeneous measures of worth, threat, and status. A single mother might worry about how she's treated at Parents' Night at school, while a single gay man might be more concerned with social discrimination or violence against homosexuals.

Making this more complex, the assumptions attached to each category of being single were in cultural flux, and they were not necessarily changing in tandem with one another. In 1958, a study found that nearly all Americans assumed a woman would stay single only if she was ugly, immoral, or neurotic. In our day we have had a range of pop-cultural portrayals, from those in *Ally McBeal* and *Judging Amy* to the vamps of *Sex in the City* and *Temptation Island*. The stereotype has changed at least in one respect: We no longer assume that single women are ugly. Single women are now the standard bearers for beauty. This is a change, for sure, but are single women still burdened with the stigma of being immoral or neurotic? Depending on which examples you pick from the media, you could argue it either way.

The decision of the *Friends* character Rachel to become a single mother, for example, appeared to be a significant step forward in the destigmatization of single motherhood. The turn in the story line did not, after all, elicit the conservative outcry that accompanied Murphy Brown's decision to do the same thing ten years ago. Indeed, NBC, ABC, WB, and HBO have all recently introduced story lines that included women who had chosen to have children on their own. The popularity of these television stories might indeed make it easier for a single mom to stand up and be heard at the next PTA meeting. But while she might sense a meaningful lessening of the stigma surrounding single motherhood, it seems unlikely that her victory advanced Coleman's status as a single gay man.

How Stereotypes Play in the Real World

I once wrote an article about a Stanford researcher who had developed a theory called "stereotype threat." He taught me that stereotypes acted in two ways. Most commonly, the stereotype affects a particular individual because people around the individual make a (usually negative) assumption about that person. But a stereotype can have a more insidious effect of existing in the mind of the individual as a threat. Subject an African-American student to a test said to measure intelligence, and it is likely that the stereotype of black intelligence will negatively affect his performance without any bias in the test questions. (Black students taking the same test without being warned that it measures intelligence will perform significantly better.) The stereotype impacts the black student's performance because he knows that in this situation there exists the threat of his confirming the stereotype. White persons should be able to understand the distracting effect of stereotype threat if they have ever talked about race issues in a room full of minorities. In that situation it is the white person who is under threat of the stereotype – that of being a racist. While the white person may not believe he is a racist, and no one else in the room may believe he is a racist, the white person will still stumble over his words, second-guessing everything he says in an attempt to avoid confirming the stereotype.

Which is all to say that while the larger culture may set stereotypes, those stereotypes can gain power via the subtle cues imbedded in smaller social situations. This is as true for the various categories of singles as it is for minority groups. If stereotypes can assert themselves even in situations where no one believes them, gauging whether stigmas and stereotypes are lessening at a given moment in time becomes a very complicated calculation.

But most important, the concept of stereotype threat suggests that the stereotypes take much of their power from subtle triggers in a social setting. This is perhaps why people often group with those who share similar stereotype threats. A white person, for example, doesn't have to contend with the stereotype threat of being a racist if she has only white friends, just as a forty-year-old single female doesn't have to worry about assumptions that she is flawed or damaged when she hangs out with her single girlfriends. It is only when we are forced to look at our lives from the potential assumptions of those outside our group that we begin to feel the pressure of the stereotypes and stigmas that haunt our time.

For myself, the stereotype threats surrounding being single and thirtysomething would only come into my consciousness when I drove to my childhood hometown to visit my mother and her friends. In this company I could feel the potential stereotypes fill the air. I knew that my mother's friends might suspect that:

- Being single in my thirties and living in San Francisco meant that I was gay.
- Being single in my thirties meant that I might be single forever.
- Living with roommates in my thirties meant that I was a slacker.

I never knew for sure if any of my mother's friends actually had these suspicions about me, but I knew the threat of these stereotypes was in the air because I could watch myself actively trying to keep them at bay. In conversations I would mention my current or most recent girlfriend to deflect the notion that I was gay. I would brag about my accomplishments and those of my friends to prove that we weren't slackers.

It wasn't that I was playacting or presenting a false self, and it wasn't that much of a hardship to emphasize certain parts of my life and personality. But as I drove back to my tribe of friends in San Francisco, I could feel the need to deflect those assumptions lift. (I could only imagine the relief a gay man would feel coming home to the Castro in San Francisco or the West Village in New York after visiting his hometown in Idaho or Mississippi.) The feeling of coming home to my urban tribe was the feeling of stepping back into the comfort of my own skin.

Our deepest sense of feeling comfortable with ourselves does not come from within, as popular New Age thinking would have us believe. Our most fundamental feelings about our self-worth come from our social situation. And by "social situation" I am not talking about the cultural norms or pop-cultural narratives that exist on a national level; rather, I mean the social situation composed by the people one actually talks to or comes within arm's reach of in a given week. Most yet-to-be-marrieds I knew lived in a social microculture to such an extent that the national zeitgeist was felt only as a small shifting of the breeze. It didn't hugely matter how being single was portrayed in the press or in television shows, the most important fact in my sense of being single was that among my friends it was considered normal.

The Single Singles

Because the various stigmas of being single existing in the culture at large could be easily deflected by one's close social circle, there was only one category of singleness that seemed like it might be a truly crushing burden: the single person who lacked not only a romantic partner but a supportive social group as well.

I did not know how large a population of single people lived without a supportive social circle. By definition you don't meet them at parties or through friends of friends. This was the category that the man I'm calling Cliff undoubtedly fell into. As we sat in the AASP office that afternoon, Cliff began to talk in that compulsive way that suggested he hadn't had the chance to talk to other people in some time. Once he started, he seemed incapable of stopping. He told us about a trip he took to Australia in 1962, about his heart condition, about his thoughts on the public transportation system in L.A., and about what it was like to make a career of teaching traffic school.

"You know," he volunteered at one point, "we're missing *Oprah* for this."

"How did you come to volunteer for the AASP?" I asked Cliff.

"I found them yesterday while I was going through the yellow pages," he said, not indicating whether he was looking for something else at the time or simply reading from page to page looking for something to do. "I saw 'American Association for Single People,' and I said to myself, Hey I'm single, so I called."

And the next day he came down to volunteer his time stuffing and sorting the AASP newsletter. Cliff was never going to be the poster boy for the AASP, but Coleman, Michael, and Kat were kind to him, and so at least for today Cliff might feel the stereotype of his single life lift a little. Count it as a small victory for the AASP.

"I volunteer for some other organizations, too," Cliff told me then. "I help out with a smoker rights group and I've never even smoked."

Chapter 6

MEN AND THE MARRIAGE DELAY
(MY HUNT FOR A GOOD EXCUSE)

You better run. You better hide.
You better lock your house and keep the kids inside.
Here comes the twentieth century's latest scam,
He's half a boy and half a man.

—Nick Lowe

A female friend of mine, a bright and attractive women's rights attorney, used to spend hours talking with me about courtship in our time. I felt privileged to be one of those guys who was articulate and empathic enough to interest a woman as smart as Samantha in such a conversation. These discussions were both fun and deeply instructive. Through hearing the stories that women share about their romantic lives, I learned volumes about what women admired and despised about men and relationships.

In many of these conversations we puzzled over the question of why relationships were not ending at the altar. It was Samantha's belief that the responsibility lay largely on the man's side of the court. Men were acting strangely cagey and often demonstrating an almost comical aversion to long-term commitments, she had observed. To illustrate this opinion, she told me an anecdote one Sunday while we were sitting in a coffee shop on Haight Street.

The story involved a woman who had been going out with a guy for a few months. After a dozen dates or so, the couple had begun the routine of sleeping together at the end of their twice-weekly nights out. All in all, the woman felt things were going along nicely, but she didn't want the momentum to plateau or stall. They had come to the well-known what's-going-on-here moment when some feelings and expectations needed to be spoken out loud.

The woman's desire to have a discussion about their relationship was not any sort of ultimatum, Samantha recounted. She wasn't interested in having *the* Talk – that is, the conversation during which one was expected to lay bare one's deepest plans and hopes for the relationship. Rather, she simply wanted to have *a* talk. The woman, you see, hadn't totally fallen for the guy. Apparently, he was something of a social klutz, which she found alternately charming and frustrating, as when he failed in simple tasks such as calling to check in the day after they had sex. Nevertheless, she felt like it was a good time to get some feelings and thoughts out on the table. She wanted to address, for one, the question of whether they were going to date each other exclusively, at least until they figured out what sort of romantic potential existed between them.

From the onset of their talk, according to Samantha, the guy was as uncomfortable as a cat on a leash. He squirmed, fidgeted, tried to change the topic, and had a hard time meeting her eyes.

"So finally the woman asked him something like 'So, what do you think?'" Samantha recounted. "After stumbling around with half-sentences which ended in 'um, know what I mean?' he finally came up with this gem: he says, 'It's not like you can have one hundred percent of me. You can maybe have fifty-one percent of me. But of that fifty-one percent, you can have one hundred percent.'"

At the punch line Samantha burst out laughing, and I tried to laugh along.

"Needless to say, she chose to have zero percent of one hundred percent of fifty-one percent," she said after regaining her composure. "What was the moron thinking?"

Thankfully, it was a rhetorical question. As it turned out, I knew pretty much exactly what he was thinking, because I was that very moron. Three weeks before, I had said those exact words to the woman I had been dating for a short time.

As Samantha went on to deride the man in the story, I tried calculating how this story had gone from my recent quasi-ex-girlfriend to Samantha. As far as I knew, they had no acquaintances in common except for myself, and I could determine no direct vectors for the spread of the tale. Given that the story had reached Samantha stripped of my identity, I could assume that it went through at least one or two retellings by people who didn't know me. I concluded that this story had spread like a minor urban legend, from woman to woman, until it got to Samantha and back to me. I was experiencing the exhilarating moment when the hero in the scary movie looks into the bathroom mirror and discovers, fangs growing and hair spouting, that the monster is he.

I did not admit my role in the story to Samantha, but I did ask her why she was repeating the story in the first place. Certainly the story had not been repeated around town because it was shocking or outrageous. As Samantha explained, the story expressed not an extreme example of male idiocy in our time, but rather the epitome of male idiocy in our time. It was being repeated because many women had vaguely experienced the thing that it revealed with sharp clarity. The story revealed, as best I could gather from Samantha, these truths and truisms:

1. There exists a depressing reality behind the cliché that men are often grossly inarticulate in situations when they are expected to talk about their feelings and expectations for a relationship.
2. Men think that the early stage of a relationship (the point at which routine sexual access is achieved with the lowest possible commitment of time, resources, and personal energy) is a fine place for the relationship to remain indefinitely.
3. A man tends to overestimate his importance to a woman at the moment when she asks him to assess the relationship. Simply put: At these moments, men often assume that the woman has fallen in love with him.

4. Men overrate the value of their affection – regardless of its quality, consistency, or certainty. That is, men often assume that a fraction of their affection (in this case, a generous and apparently controlling share of 51 percent) is so valuable that it might represent a whole of something (hence 100 percent of 51 percent).

5. Men's tendency toward grandiosity combined with their inability to articulate their intentions reveals them to be the most reprehensible of cowards. After all, if men so readily perceive themselves to be the be-all and end-all at the moment when the woman wants to know what is going on in a relationship (see number 3), shouldn't that grand self-conception carry along with it some responsibilities for addressing the situation with candor, clarity, and honor?

6. Men often ride along in romantic relationships with one hand on the door handle. This fearfulness of momentum leads them to perform all measure of foolishness, including dangerous stuntman-like dives out of high-speed romances as well as more comical leaps out of relationships that have yet to leave the driveway.

I think it was my inarticulateness that was the most disturbing part of the story. As I mentioned above, when discussing other people's romances I could sometimes show an uncanny ability to discern intentions, parse out emotions, and make meaning. To my friend Samantha, I played the upstanding, emotionally articulate man I believed myself to be. That I could have simultaneously been that thoughtful guy friend and the commitment-phobic stereotype of her story was disconcerting and mildly dissociative. There was no getting around the fact that I had some explaining to do to myself.

Most of the men I knew were also in the position of desiring a reason for their behavior. This is not to say that I was friends with men who cruelly gamed women for sex. Like me, the men I knew had deep respect for women and were capable of empathy. Yet at the end of their romantic relationships, they were more likely than the women they dated to feel some guilt – some sense that they had screwed it up. The women I knew, on the other hand, were more likely to come out of relationships on the moral high ground, even if they were the ones who dumped the guy. They usually seemed to have good reasons for getting out of relationships whether it was an emotional disconnect or a lack of long-term compatibility.

Men's motivations for getting out were harder (sometimes impossible) to defend. Men were more likely to bail out of some vague sense that they needed their "freedom," which was often code for their desire to pursue some fantasy of a perfect mate. Or sometimes they fled relationships out of a desire not to find one perfect mate but to sleep with many imperfect ones. Sometimes men didn't even know why they wanted out. The stakes in understanding my own motivations were as steep as they come. After so many years of singleness, it was becoming increasingly difficult to look myself in the mirror and believe that I was capable of true love. The women I dated were smart, charming, and attractive. There was only one constant variable in all those failures – me. That stark fact would sometimes keep me awake late into the night.

But in the light of day, to believe such a thing about yourself is difficult. The human animal is remarkably adept at seeing itself as the hero, no matter what the story. When we act badly or fail, our brains work to supply us with as all the exemptions and rationales we need to turn the moral of the story on its head. Certain excuses were easy: I dropped the ball because the sun was in my eyes. However, when you've dropped every ball that's ever come your way, you have to be more creative in your excuses.

Pilgrimage to the Experts

It was on the hunt for a reason/excuse for my behavior that, in the middle 1990s, I voluntarily spent four days with eighteen thousand therapists and psychological researchers at the American Psychological Association's annual convention. Midtown Manhattan had been virtually taken over by bright-eyed members of the caring profession, who were swarming through eighteen hotels from Forty-second Street up to Central Park and milling through Times Square without the sense to take off their nametags. I had come to this particular convention because a cadre of therapists and researchers had recently turned their attention to the tribulations particular to being a man in modern-day America. The APA had created a new branch: Division 51, which focused exclusively on the troubling behavior of men. In the index of the program – which was the size of a phone book – I found that Division 51 listed six scheduled events. (By contrast under Women's Studies there were more than sixty seminars.) I headed toward the first, titled "Recent Advances in the Psychotherapy of Men."

There were four men seated at a table to the right of the podium – all could have been cast as the science teacher in a high school sitcom; all had wedding rings. William Pollack, coauthor of *In a Time of Fallen Heroes: The Re-Creation of Masculinity*, began the proceedings with a pronouncement about the origin of male unhappiness.

"Boys suffer a premature psychic break from their maternal and paternal caregivers," he began, as if everyone already knew and accepted this fact. "This puts them at risk of creating a defensive self-sufficiency later in life." I took that to mean that boys were told too early to stop showing childish emotion and, dagnabit, act like men. Because we were treated in this cruel manner, Pollack argued, we were afraid to show or express affection for fear that we'd be brutalized for our weakness. "Men are mostly afraid of being afraid," he concluded. I wrote that down in my notebook and underlined it.

The next three speakers followed along on the same theme. David Lisak, from the University of Massachusetts in Boston, told the gathering that most men had been raised with "all feminine aspects of their personality excised." Larry Morris, who was then in the process of writing *The Heterosexual Male: Lust in His Loins, Sin in His Soul?*, went next, claiming that "becoming a male in our society is like negotiating a minefield with a faulty map. One false step and boom! – your genitals of masculinity are history." Gary Brooks, author of *The Centerfold Syndrome*, followed them, suggesting that men could overcome the roadblocks of traditional masculine socialization through therapy and networking with other nurturing and supportive men. "Men must learn to do what comes unnaturally," he announced.

After the four men spoke, a female therapist took the podium and began patting them all on the head. She said that we must all understand, but not excuse, men for becoming the "monsters of feminist nightmares" because of the damaging process of gender training, which was "sometimes brutal, always dehumanizing." Men must be pitied, she told us, because we were brought up as only "half-persons."

What a bonanza! These were just the sort of excuses I had traveled three thousand miles to hear. It was because of early psychological scars that so many men of my generation – including myself – were seemingly incapable of forming long-lasting romantic relationships. That night I called my mother in California to tell her how she had emotionally crippled me as a young boy, thus making me inept at bonding with women in my adult romantic life. "You stopped me from being affectionate and emotional too early," I accused.

"Ethan, you were born in Berkeley in the sixties," she said. "We were very conscious of these things. Everyone was trying to raise sexless children."

"You were trying to raise us sexless?"

"No. 'Sexless' is not the right word," she said, pausing. "You know, we all bought toy trucks for little girls and dolls for boys."

"You mean 'genderless'?"

"Right, genderless," she said. "You know, your brother had a doll."

"So you never stopped me from crying or hugging?" I asked. "Never told me to act like a man?"

"No, as I remember, you cried all you wanted," she said.

The Psychologist in the Sex Shop

On the second day of the conference, I ran into Gary Brooks, who argues in *The Centerfold Syndrome* that the selling of sex in our society has sabotaged individual relationships between men and women. Since the nearly literal intersection of sex and commerce was only a few blocks away, I talked him into walking toward Times Square. (This was the middle nineties, remember, before Mayor Rudy Giuliani completely cleaned up Times Square, turning it into a kind of theme park for advertisers and the major television networks.)

As we walked, I explained my romantic troubles. I had left good and kind-hearted women, I confessed; I could not seem to commit to one woman. Brooks, a short, balding guy of forty-nine, who exuded the jovial sincerity of a Unitarian minister, nodded with each detail. Apparently, he had heard the story before.

We arrived at one of the larger sex emporiums, and I led Brooks under the flashing lights and into a long room lined with video boxes and magazines. "Is it any surprise you have trouble focusing on one woman?" Brooks asked rhetorically, sweeping his arm across the large, well-lit room. "Look around here! Society has created a desire for constant variety – this is the reason you have such trouble maintaining a relationship."

Brooks was certainly right about one thing: the models in the magazines and on the video boxes appeared remarkably diverse. The women pictured came from all races, all postpubescent ages (although dramatically skewed toward the young and firm-fleshed – the sex videos featuring elderly women and men were shelved with the extreme fetishes), and possessed vastly, and I mean *vastly*, different physical attributes. Brooks studied the offerings with an appropriately detached, scholarly demeanor.

"The first thing you need to do in order to change is you have to stop masturbating to visual images of imaginary women. This cultural bias toward constant sexual variety is pernicious," Brooks declared, gesturing at me with a video box featuring African men having sex with Scandinavian women. "Instead, you should fantasize about sensuality, touch, and smell. In that way you can steer your desire away from the idea of variety and toward the idea of intimacy with a single lover.

"What really worries me is what gets played out there in the real world," he said. "Out there you see women parading seductively

144

around and men thinking, 'What a tempting fox, I'd like to fuck that bitch.'"

Even surrounded by such an excess of evidence (and even though I wanted to believe him), his argument that we were socialized to have nonmonogamous desires seemed pretty weak. Pop culture has told me more stories about Mr. Cleavers and Mr. Bradys than it has about Mr. Bonds. While I was growing up, the only positive portrayal on television of a guy who slept around was Captain Kirk, and his behavior was excused because he was sleeping with alien women, who, fortunately for him, were apparently exactly like human women except for their exciting skin color and sexual manners. In general, however, non-monogamous males were vilified if they could not be redeemed through the behavior-altering love of a single faithful woman. The doggedly devoted husband was the glorified norm. If I had learned my desires from cultural stories, I should be a natural lapdog.

I just wasn't convinced that my reaction to the sight of a beautiful woman was all socialization. "It seems that my blood pressure reacts to seeing pretty women without conscious request," I told him as we walked back out onto the busy street.

"That's what the culture has done to you," Brooks insisted. "You've been manipulated to have a physiological reaction to the newness. You have to try and imagine a culture in which men and women live in an egalitarian sort of life and there is no need for . . ." His words trailed off as his eyes fixed on something over my shoulder. I turned to find two twentyish Asian women in leather minidresses sauntering up the sidewalk. When I turned back, Brooks was looking a little sheepish. "Yes, it happens to me too. Like you, I've been socialized to have certain reactions. I work hard not to respond in that type of way. I try to say to myself: I don't need this."

The Excuse in My Genes

The next day I attended "Men and Sex – Biological Lust or Relational Love?," which featured several of the touchy-feely characters I heard

145

the day before. The new guy on the podium was David Buss, author of *The Evolution of Desire*, in which he argued that undying love was the exception in human coupling. Much more natural to mating, Buss suggested, were the very things we saw as love's perversions: betrayal, wayward desire, and conflict.

Buss, I had heard, was becoming the public face for the blossoming field of evolutionary psychology, the field that purported to explain human behavior in general, and sexuality in particular, through an examination of inherited psychological mechanisms and apparatuses that influenced our emotions and actions. It was clear the field could have done much worse in finding an unofficial spokesperson. In his mid-forties, Buss was tall, athletic, and square-jawed-handsome in a post-gawky, professorial sort of way. He displayed the even, confident posture of an alpha male. Buss exuded confidence as he stood next to an overhead projector and lectured to the packed room without a microphone.

Buss argued that there was trouble between the sexes because men and women, on average, had brains that came preloaded with different mating strategies and sexual desires. It was those differences that ensured conflict. As his first piece of evidence, Buss described a survey that asked men and women how many sexual partners they would ideally like to have over a series of time intervals. He tossed down a transparency showing the results. In the graph of the women's responses, the line was rather flat. On average, they preferred only eight-tenths of a sexual partner in a month, one in a year, two over three years, and just five over an average idealized lifetime. The men's line shot up at roughly the angle of an erection. On average they preferred two sexual partners in a month, five over a year, ten over three years, and twenty over a lifetime.

While this all may sound like science proving the obvious, the crucial fact was that Buss and his colleagues had been finding very similar results in every culture they'd surveyed. This suggested that such a difference in the desire for sexual variety was not taught to us through culture but was a desire that we inherited.

The next slide was equally revealing. In another survey, Buss and his

146

fellow researchers attempted to find out whether there was a difference between men and women in terms of the amount of time they wanted to elapse before they consented to having sex with an attractive member of the opposite sex. The average time for women was roughly six months after meeting the attractive man. For men it was one week. But it was the two ends of these lines that struck me as most interesting. The women's curve was still rising in likelihood between the two- and five-year marks while the men's curve was declining at that point. Some women would still be warming up to the idea of sex after two years, while the men by that point would be looking for another, more willing, attractive member of the opposite sex.

The other end of the graph was even more fascinating. For women, the amount of time before sex bottomed out at a week, meaning no women reported wanting to have sex with an attractive man after knowing him for less than a week. The men's curve, on the other hand, never bottomed out. There were many men who reported that they would be willing to consent to sex at the one-hour mark.

I thought it was a shame that one hour was the shortest time period measured in the survey, because I'm sure there would be a good number of men who would consent to sex with an attractive member of the opposite sex at the minute, second, or tenth-of-a-second mark. Of course, at that point they might have had to employ a theoretical physicist to divide time into an interval small enough to chart that end of the men's curve. According to something I saw on PBS once, the smallest parsing of an instant is the amount of time it takes light, the fastest thing in the universe, to travel across the smallest thing in the universe (a quark or something). But there would probably be some men who would be even faster than that, because they would have consented to sex *before having met* the attractive woman. Some men would have consented to sex with an attractive woman, unilaterally and for all future time, somewhere back in junior high.

Regardless, according to Buss, the study showed that it was "very clear that men have a greater desire for short-term sexual strategies than women do."

As the lecture went on, the importance of Buss's work became more and more meaningful to me. The difficulties my friends and I had in settling on one woman, it seemed, had less to do with our personal choices than with our inherited desires. Unlike the rest of the speakers, Buss, as I understood him then, argued that the key to understanding behavior was not in examining what we've been taught, but in understanding what we were – male animals with instincts and inherited proclivities that often cruelly conflicted with the instincts and inherited proclivities of the female animals we dated.

After the seminar I cornered Buss, desperate to know the type of mating strategy that most closely mirrored our evolutionary propensities. "For women," he said, "I think if you just looked at their inherited desires, they would be attracted to tall, physically fit men who displayed confidence, status, and the potential to be resource providers."

"But what about men?" I asked. "What if there were no religion or laws regulating sexual behavior. What would men want?"

"I think in that case men would want a polygamous lifestyle – multiple wives." Buss said. "Polygamy combines the best features of short-term and long-term strategies. For the men who are in the position to lead quasi-polygamous lives, like kings and emperors, that is exactly what they do."

"But our society doesn't allow polygamy," I protested. "The chances that I'll become polygamous are about as good as the chances someone is going to appoint me king of France. If that's what my brain wants, how will I ever be happy? How come we've made rules against it?"

At this question, Buss began to edge away from me, a little taken aback to learn that I was on a personal quest. "Well, monogamy is probably enforced because society is mostly composed of beta males," Buss explained. "It's tough to get elected by a population of beta males if people know that you're going to have a thousand young women in your harem. In polygamous systems, some men get left out, so it's in the beta males' best interest to make rules about monogamy."

Before Buss shifted his attention to one of the fawning graduate students who were closing in on him, he took pity on me. "Look, evolution didn't create the human animal to be happy," he said, as if that would be reassuring. "We're not designed to reach a continuous state of happiness. Evolution created in humans an animal who always wants more."

Conversation Starters I Wish I'd Stopped

This brief introduction to David Buss and his theories of evolutionary psychology coincided, not coincidentally, with my years of getting into arguments with my women friends. This was how it would usually go down: At a party, a woman from my urban tribe would tell a story about a man saying or doing something reprehensible in a romantic relationship. As everyone else would shake their heads in disbelief at the man's behavior, I would mention that according to evolutionary psychology, such behavior was predictable.

"Predictable, hell," the women would counter. "That guy acted like a jerk."

"Yes, well, if you understood evolutionary psychology to the depths that I understand it," I would say, "you would know that men and women have different inherited desires and that conflict is inevitable."

I would then tell everyone listening just how women and men differed in their desires. A man, I would tell them, prefers a mating strategy that includes a good amount of sexual variety, while a woman was more likely to be monogamous. Then, after telling them that men were naturally attracted to youth and beauty and that women were attracted to resource providers, all hell would break loose. As the argument began, my male friends would usually move away, suddenly showing interest in the snack table or the Monet posters on the wall. When I was alone, the women would circle in.

The first thing that women would refuse to concede was that men and women differed in their sexual desires at all. Interestingly, this denial often took the form of their insistence that women were every

149

bit as sexually omnivorous as I suggested men were. In particular, they claimed that women were every bit as likely to desire sex outside of relationships and desire sexual variety. "If I was ovulating, I'd want to fuck every guy in this room," a female friend of mine said to me during one of these debates.

"Have you ever had sex with every guy at a party while you were ovulating?" I asked.

"No, of course not," she said. "But I'd *want* to."

I didn't believe her (and I still don't). I'd never, in person, witnessed a woman behave that way. Either there were not many of them or they were attending parties to which I was not invited. The fact that we could not even agree that women and men differed (on average) in their desire for sexual variety meant the debate often got stuck at the starting line.

Sometimes, my female opponents would agree that men and women *acted* differently. They would quickly concede that men were more likely to leave relationships for nefarious reasons and they allowed that middle-aged men were more likely to leave their spouses if an attractive twenty-year-old became available to them. They would even point out that men, on average, were more likely than women to be interested in buying sex from strangers, more likely to drool over sexually explicit pictures, and more likely to be convicted of all manner of sex crimes. They would concede, in short, that when it came to sexual behavior, men could be counted on to act more poorly than women.

This was not exactly a victory for my side, but it did provide a wedge by which I could advance my point. Why, I would ask, did men act more despicably when it came to sexual matters? Certainly not because of inherited sexual desires, my women friends would insist. This led them to the conclusion that was usually the essence of their argument: If women had the same desires as men but generally behaved better, this proved that women were *choosing* to behave better, thus giving them the moral high ground from which they could blame men for *choosing* to act badly.

When pushed, these women sometimes conceded that personal choice wasn't the only factor influencing the sexual behavior of men and women. "Cultural influences," they said, might also be to blame. This turned out only to be a strategic concession, for blaming culture or socialization still left bad behavior in the province of choice. If we learned this way of acting, we should we be able to unlearn it as well.

In addition, since it was okay to blame men for every horrible thing created in a patriarchal culture – from short hemlines and *Playboy* magazine to the ubiquitous influence of advertising to the stereotype of the fifties housewife – then we men had only ourselves to blame. In fact, if men were learning our twisted desires through culture or socialization, then we were doubly at fault: first for the way we behaved and second for teaching ourselves that it was okay to behave in that manner.

Pretty much every woman I argued with had a visceral negative reaction to the idea that certain desires came prelearned in our brains. I suppose it was understandable. It's certainly more reassuring to believe that problematic sexual desires were a curable neurosis, or a sign of someone's immaturity, or an outgrowth of capitalism. Besides, the evolutionary psychological theories I offered were nothing but bad news for women growing into their middle adulthood. If men were inherently attracted to youthful, attractive, and fertile women, then I was basically arguing that these female friends of mine were losing their mate value as they aged – even if they simultaneously grew more confident, intelligent, and successful.

As If I Hadn't Gone Far Enough

When these arguments came around to the evolutionary psychological theory that men might naturally prefer polygamy to monogamy, the argument would get downright unpleasant.

"What about women?" they would ask. "Could high-status women have multiple husbands?"

"Of course not," I would say. "Evolutionary psychology tells us that women are more comfortable with monogamy."

"Women would want to be monogamous with a man who was polygamous? Bullshit," they would counter. "What's fair about that?"

"Given that men and women have dramatically different biological functions in procreation, it wouldn't make sense that things were 'fair,'" I would explain. "A polygamous system would suit both men and women. Women could be happy being sexually loyal to one resource-providing man while the man could be happy having sex with his many wives."

At this point things would often go silent for a minute. Some women would stare at me, jaws agape, while others glanced around the room for candlesticks and paperweights and other hefty objects that might be used to beat some sense into me. When they found their tongues again, they would tell me how ludicrous it was that I would even consider that women would be interested in such a blatantly inequitable setup.

After that these women "friends" would usually begin to mock me with ad hominem attacks on my personal-mate value. Instead of making a legitimate argument to counter my vision of a polygamous paradise, they would stoop to suggest that in such a setup, there wouldn't be enough women to go around for idiots like myself. I would be left to sleep alone, they would tell me, while they would end up in Mark Wahlberg's harem. Then they would laugh and laugh.

Outright ridicule tended to win the day. I believed they used it both to humiliate me and as an effective way to counter what they perceived to be the true subtext of my argument. In the end they thought that my evolutionary-psychology theories were nothing more than a intellectual excuse for any bad behavior as well as a fertile ground for some lingering adolescent harem fantasies.

They were right, of course, and their laughter abruptly dismantled these fantasies in the way nuclear bombs dismantled houses. It is hard to underestimate the power of mockery to win a debate on gender and sexual behavior. Their derision carried the unmistakable and deeply affecting message: "You silly little man, don't think for a second that your silly little theories are going to let you get away with any shenanigans."

At the end of these debates, I would slink off as the women continued to snicker. Later, alone at home, I would read more evolutionary psychology and wait for the next party with new arguments at the ready. But it would always end the same way, and after a while I would be invited to dinners and parties only on the condition that I not expound my theories of differential mating strategies. Eventually, I had to face one disturbing fact: My knowledge of evolutionary psychology was having a negative impact on my interactions with my female friends.

And not only with friends. The few times that I tried to describe my evolutionary-psychology theories to a woman I was dating were some of the most awkward and depressing moments I've experienced in my time on the planet. What was I thinking? Even with my penchant for self-mockery, I cannot bring myself to recount these sad occasions. In the hopes of stopping any man from following in my footsteps, let me be clear: Evolutionary psychology may be a tool for understanding mating strategies, but it is not itself a mating strategy. It may, in fact, be the opposite of a mating strategy.

In my disastrous attempts to explain evolutionary psychology, I usually had the feeling that I didn't know quite enough about its theories to defend them. Given that I had yet to win one of these debates, I was left with two choices: Either stop talking about the theories altogether, or go back to my original source and gather the arguments I needed to win the day.

A Night on the Town with an Evolutionary Psychologist

So it came to be that I went to meet Professor David Buss again, this time in his hometown of Austin, Texas, on a windy spring evening. Buss had picked the nightclub-lined Sixth Street because he promised to critique for me the evolved mating styles of the twentysomething human. "I've been studying human mating for so long, I do sometimes feel that I've become an anthropologist in my own culture," he said, as we peered in the window of a bar. "It is pretty clear to me when someone is flirting or trying to evoke jealousy."

At the first club the pickings were slim. The night was young, and the mating dances were still tentative and not yet loosened by alcohol. Finally, Buss spotted a young couple talking and laughing near a pool table in a quiet lounge. There was clearly some chemistry between the two, but it was Buss who broke the hidden code of their sexual attraction.

"Note the female's shiny hair and symmetrical facial features. Males like those signs of health and fertility," said Buss. "Good hip-to-waist ratio, too."

The male, tall, puff-chested, and holding a pool cue, also had a few things going for him. Buss noted his new clothes and nice watch, which signaled "resource acquisition potential" that women were inherently prone to dig. Then there was the pool cue, which, according to Buss, required no elaborate Freudian interpretation. In Buss's conception, the pool cue was simply the component of a game through which men compete for status and hence access to shiny-haired, symmetrical women.

It was a lovely little tableau, these two attractive human specimens laughing, flirting, and touching. Unfortunately, as Buss went on to tell me, the future of this couple was less than hopeful. Sure, things might go well that night and the following weeks or even for the next couple of months or years, but at some point the male would likely be plagued with desire for variety in his sexual partners. The female would keep an eye out for available males with higher social status, which would make her partner seethe with jealous, perhaps violent, thoughts. They were unlikely to avoid these pitfalls, Buss explained, as the seeds of conflict and misery were preprogrammed into their psychological natures.

"Much of what I've discovered about human mating is not nice," Buss said. "Men and women deceive each other and torture each other both physically and emotionally. Human nature has many dark sides. I wish these aspects of human nature didn't exist, but they do."

On that cheery thought, I ordered a beer. Buss's disclaimer, which was much like the last thing he had said to me years before in New York, seemed now a touch disingenuous. He might have wished such troubles didn't exist between the sexes, but he certainly seemed to get a kick out of pointing them out. His reputation for exposing the evolved psychological mechanisms that predispose us to conflict in our mating and social lives had gotten him on a lot of talk shows over the years. While that didn't mean he was an advocate for these unfortunate aspects of human nature, he certainly appeared to enjoy turning the light on the cockroaches in the kitchen of the human psyche.

When I suggested that he might like the fight he was in – that he might enjoy pointing out that we as a species were pretty much doomed to rocky mating lives – he vehemently disagreed.

"I've been the target of some really vicious attacks," said Buss. "That's certainly not very fun. The people who really hate my work expect me to be a monster and are surprised that I don't have horns. You don't get this sort of debate in chemistry. Chemists don't go around shouting at each other, 'Take back that thing you said about the boron molecule!' I try to present my evidence, and what I often get back is ad hominem attacks on my character, distortions of what I've said, or just shrillness and emotion."

Having tried to champion his theories, I knew something of the persecution he had suffered. I imagined that both Buss and I were truth-telling rebels, like Galileo, fighting against the orthodoxies of our time.

"Has your experience arguing the tenets of evolutionary psychology made you less attractive to women?" I asked, adding in my mind, "It certainly has for me."

"Actually, not at all," he said. "The work has given me status, and that makes men desirable. If I give a talk in front of a large audience and it's successful, women come up afterward. I've even had fairly direct sexual advances from women who will say something like, 'I really don't like your work, but would you like to have a drink later?' "

I was curious to learn more about how his theories guided his personal romantic life, but for the most part Buss was unwilling to answer those questions. Public discussion of his love life was a touchy subject with Buss for good reason. Some critics, he said, have assumed that his theories hide an advocacy for his personal behavior. His hypothesis that humans are very rarely happily monogamous for a lifetime is, for instance, sometimes taken as evidence that Buss advocates and practices nonmonogamous behavior.

"I don't get it. Some people think that because of what I've published I sleep around all the time. I don't," he said. "I have the same inherited psychological mechanisms that everyone else does, but I don't think my theories have affected my personal mating life."

Buss was particularly sensitive about the notion that he was advocating any behavior, and he cringed at the thought that there might be people somewhere who had evoked his research to justify nefarious mating tactics or acting on every desire. "When people hear the word 'evolution,' people think 'determinism'," he said, shaking his head in wonder, "and they think that I'm providing a justification for behavior or that I'm arguing that it is inevitable that we're doomed to the world of conflict that we have."

Uh-oh, I thought. This misstep sounded familiar.

"Of course," I said. "And those misguided people would be making a mistake because . . ."

"Because none of that is true," he said. "Evolutionary theory does not interfere with trying to find love or trying to making the world a better place. On the contrary, if our goal as a society is to, say, stop violence against women or ameliorate excessive competitiveness among men or be monogamous, then it is essential that we understand the underlying evolved psychology that is influencing our desires."

"So our evolved psychological adaptation shouldn't dictate how we act?"

"No mating behavior is inevitable or preordained," Buss said, sound-

156

ing exasperated, although it wasn't clear whether it was with me or with the legions of people he had met in the past who seemed to willfully misread and mishear his argument. "The problem is that people tend to have a cartoonist version for what it means to assert that something is an evolved adaptation. All individuals, men and women, have a range of mating strategies that are highly complex, highly situation dependent, and they only manifest themselves with certain complex contextual input. Influenced by our particular situations, we very much choose which strategy to pursue and which to keep dormant. It is not the case that men are lust-filled sexual predators and that women just want long-term monogamous relationships. Women sometimes have a lot of lust and want causal sexual encounters, and sometimes they want the long-term mate commitment. People don't seem to want to understand the complexity here. If I say that there is a psychological mechanism for men to sometimes adopt short-term mating strategies, then people think I'm saying that men should sleep around. That's just stupid. We are not slaves to any particular sexual role created by evolution."

"It must be difficult to have your theories go out into the world and be misrepresented by people who only half-understand them," I said.

"Yes, it is. Evolutionary psychology is a complicated field of study," Buss said, cooling down a little. "When people talk to physicists, they don't think to offer their own theories about quantum mechanics. But weirdly, that is not true with evolutionary psychology. Even after reading a couple of superficial magazine articles about it, people go around thinking they understand it."

Looked at one way, I thought to myself, he only had himself to blame. It was his decision, after all, to introduce the public to evolutionary psychology at the same time it was forming as a discipline. If you allow the general population onto your team, you shouldn't be surprised that your team is going to end up including a large number of boneheads unacclimatized to heights of evolutionary reasoning. That his most ardent advocates, like myself, would make mistakes as they argued for what they thought were the precepts of this new science might have been predicted.

The Road to Contrition Not Taken

Back home in San Francisco, I decided not to apologize or clarify my position to the various women I had argued with over the previous years. It was clear I had drawn a number of fanciful conclusions from the little I had thought I understood about evolutionary psychology, but their stubborn unwillingness to concede even the possibility that men and women, on average, have different evolved propensities made me disinclined toward contrition. If they refused to budge, I would too. Anyway, I had already experienced enough humiliation by floating my assumptions – why add to my burden by changing my position? Easier just to bring up the subject no longer.

I had made the mistake of getting carried away with one piece of data – namely, that men and women differed on average in their sexual desires for variety and interest in engaging in short-term sexual strategies. From that oh-so-obvious fact, I drew all sorts of nitwit conclusions; primary among them was the assumption that the world would be a better place and I would be a happier person if more women would allow me to succeed in using short-term mating strategies. Nothing, and I mean *nothing*, about evolutionary psychology pointed toward this conclusion. In fact, no respectable evolutionary psychologist I knew of had attempted to make a correlation between any particular mating strategy and greater or lesser degrees of happiness for those who employed them.

It was clear, in fact, that all strategies would inevitably involve some level of rivalry, acrimony between the sexes, and mixed feelings among one's own sometimes conflicting desires. Yes, the social world I lived in required the continual sublimation of certain impulses, but to imagine a world in which men were allowed to have sex with women spontaneously (or allowed to hoard multiple partners for themselves) was to imagine a frantic place where jealousy and bitter male competition would be even more pronounced. Would I really wish for that reality to exist? Worse yet, a world in which short-term mating strategies were the norm would be a world in which our evolved desire for long-term partnerships would be the yearning that had to be sublimated.

At the end of my enthusiasm with evolutionary psychology, I knew little more about human mating than I had already known. I hadn't needed this burgeoning discipline to tell me that lifelong happy human couplings were few and far between. The fact that love was hard to find and hard to maintain was something I already understood from looking at the relationships around me.

I also knew that desires (between men and women or even within one's own psyche) ebbed and flowed and often came into grave conflict with each other. I could turn on any sitcom and find extended (if not deep) variations on this truth. I already knew that in the strictest sense of the word, humans were not monogamous. After all, no one I knew, including myself, had managed a perpetual devotion to only one mate. At most, the people I knew were serial monogamists who maintained the hope that their current (or very next) romance would last the distance.

Some evolutionary psychologists implied that the public's penchant for dismissing evolutionary psychology hid a cowardly unwillingness to fully understand ourselves in the cold clear light of science. They were probably right. But there was something else in the mix, too. Our ability to disconnect our emotions and desires from their mechanisms might be as much an act of courage as wishful thinking. I wanted to believe that the love I was searching for would be a singular experience. I did not want to think about my "mating strategies" or my selfish genes struggling to perpetuate themselves into the next generation.

But my biggest mistake of all was assuming that evolutionary psychology had anything to tell me about why I hadn't gotten married. Given that other generations had more success with getting married younger and keeping those marriages going longer, it seemed clear the secret to my generation's marriage delay did not lie in evolutionary psychology. Yes, I had pursued relatively short-term mating strategies, but I had done so by choice, not because I had been hardwired to behave in a certain way.

The Case for Love

Critics of evolutionary psychology often point to the remarkable spectrum of human creativity as a rebuttal to the idea that we are narrowly constructed to advance our genes. If we are simply out to procreate successfully, they ask, how does one explain those who devote themselves to creating great works of literature, science, architecture, art, and music? Why do humans desire to sing the praises of the universe with whatever talent they happen to possess?

Of course, the evolutionary psychologists have their answer. They say that showing creativity is a complex mating display – our peacock's tail, so to speak. Such creativity is the way in which humans achieve status and demonstrate that their genes carry intelligence.

But even if Beethoven's reason for creating his Ninth Symphony was to gain status and impress the babes, the work achieved something that transcended his human drives. It was within this paradox – that humans could create something noble even as they were driven by their ignoble instincts – that I found some hope for love. It occurred to me that our human ability to create something meaningful and lasting might be applied to the making of a single romantic relationship. Certainly, the human intellect had worse uses (improvisational dance, a cappella singing, and arguing evolutionary psychology at dinner parties came immediately to mind). I didn't see any reason why we couldn't release romantic relationships from their connection with our evolutionary propensities and put them into the more open landscape of our peculiar human desire to create something beautiful. A romantic relationship built as a two-person masterwork of human intelligence and creativity seemed, at least theoretically, possible.

Chapter 7

WOMEN AND THE MARRIAGE DELAY

Things that change precipitously from one generation to the next are usually greeted by the older generation as the death of everything good and right. This was certainly true of the fact that a whole cohort of women were not getting married as promptly as their mothers did. The facts were certainly dramatic: The proportion of never-married women between twenty and twenty-four had doubled in thirty years, while in the same time the proportion of never-marrieds between thirty and thirty-four had tripled. With the swelling pitch of civic emergency sirens, men and women of religious and political virtue stepped forward, as the millennium turned, to express their deep concern, outrage, and/or indignation over this trend.

The fact that fully 40 percent of adult females were single proved that we were suffering a "titanic loss of family values," wrote Robert Stacy McCain in the *Washington Times*, adding that today's young women appeared "indifferent to traditional notions of marriage and morality." We must allocate more resources to understand these trends, wrote Rutgers researchers (who, coincidentally, benefited from the resources allocated to understand these trends), because marriage "contributes to the physical, emotional and economic health of men, women and children, and thus to the nation as a whole." An article in *Time* magazine asked whether "picky" women would end up "denying themselves and society the benefits of marriage," and wondered excitedly whether this would mean "an outbreak of *Sex in the City* promiscuity."

Scurrilous politicians, looking for easy scapegoats, went as far as blaming these women for the imminent demise of Western civilization. Absent "the sudden desire on the part of Western women to begin having the same-sized families as their grandmothers, the future belongs to the Third World," Patrick J. Buchanan writes in his book *The Death of the West*. "Only the mass reconversion of Western women to an idea that they seem to have given up – that the good life lies in bearing and raising children and sending them out into the world to continue the family and nation – can prevent the Death of the West."*

In the first years of the new millennium, anger and distrust of these women ran like a low-grade fever throughout our culture. When articles came out about thirtysomething women who worried about finding someone to marry, they got little sympathy. These women were falling prey to the "perfect-person problem," reported Michael Broder, a psychotherapist and author of *The Art of Living Single*. In waiting for the perfect man, they were overlooking men with whom they might be happy if they gave the relationship a chance to develop.

Similarly, when surveys of these mature single women revealed that a significant number of them still hoped to have children, reporters from magazines, newspapers, and television shows nearly trampled each other to deliver the news that fertility starts its most dramatic decline at thirty. How could these women, the commentary accompanying this news went, have thought that they could ignore nature? ("nature" meaning the biology of conception but also, I think, slyly implying a "woman's nature," i.e., as a mother). It took no reading between the lines to see a smirking satisfaction at the news that these women would pay for having turned their back on marriage and family for too long.

---

* "Western women," "our civilization," "people of European Stock" – Buchanan goes out of his way to find phrases to hint at what he seems to mean: white people. The worse-case scenario he seems to be presenting is not that the human population will decline, but that Europe and America are going to be overrun by non-Europeans. Of course he never makes a direct case for why this is so terrible or why nonwhites could not further "Western civilization." His outrage implies that all right-thinking people already know the answers to these questions.

Are These the Women We Hate?

I met Beth at a coffee shop in Philadelphia when she was a couple of months away from her thirtieth birthday. Associate director of student affairs at the Wharton School of the University of Pennsylvania, Beth had strong shoulders and the confident giat of an athlete. She had dark hair that was simply cut at medium length, and she was pretty, with a bit of tomboy in her carriage and manner. She possessed an unassuming older-sisterly confidence that I was sure made her popular among the students she counseled.

Given how Beth presented herself, I immediately made the assumption that she had turned down many men over her years of being single and that those rejects were probably men just like me. I don't know where those two ideas came from, but a chain of thoughts like a muscle reflex quickly followed them. I found myself suddenly thinking that if Beth had been meeting me for a blind date and not a journalistic interview, she would already be making an excuse to end it early, giving me some pretext about her big important job, no doubt. What was so wrong with me? So I wasn't the handsomest guy on the block, and yes, I had some commitment "issues," but women like Beth just didn't stick around long enough to see through my flaws. *Of course she hadn't found someone to marry, with a stuck-up attitude like that . . .*

My brain managed to rattle though these thoughts in the amount of time that it took me to take a sip of my coffee. This virulent defensiveness obviously had nothing to do with Beth's actual romantic choices: I had just met her and knew almost nothing about her life. Coming to my senses, I wondered whether my knee-jerk reaction partially explained our culture's suspicion of women in Beth's position. Were single women in their late twenties and up taking such heat because they catalyzed men's insecurities? It was easy to assume that women like Beth had rejected many suitors, and if no one had been good enough so far, it's not hard to make the leap that you wouldn't be, either. (This insecurity is particularly virulent when watching ultra-attractive women play single characters on television. When he watches *Sex and the City*, Patrick Buchanan knows that he would never get a second look from the likes of Sarah Jessica Parker, and I can imagine that that makes him even more bitter and broken inside. "This is the death of Western civilization," he mutters to himself as he continues to watch.) If these women are going to reject us, we might as well get the jump on them by questioning their character and worth first.

My initial defensiveness faded quickly. I was reacting to a stereotype of who I thought Beth was, but as I learned more about her life, it became impossible to typecast her as a woman too picky for her own good.

Given her early career success at the university, I was not surprised to learn of the trail of successes that went back to her college days. At Rosemont College in Pennsylvania, she was class president three years running and then student-body president her senior year in addition to captain of the field hockey team. Rosemont was a small all-girls Catholic school, and she was the star among the six hundred students. Within the structure of college she seemed to lead a charmed life, succeeding at almost everything she tried.

Her years directly after college were not as easy. Once out in the world of endless choices, she kind of froze up. She couldn't seem to figure out what to do next. After being at the top of the food chain in college, starting again among the filter feeders seemed like a letdown. Devoted to her family, she went home to figure out what to do and ended up waiting tables for a year.

"It was kind of a horrible freedom. No one tells you how hard that time of life is going to be," she told me. "It was pretty unsettling for someone who had always been a leader and always had a goal to suddenly be confused about what to do next. You feel like you are letting down your friends and family and anyone who had ever believed in you."

For a time, she returned to the scene of her glory years. Rosemont hired her back as an admissions officer, and not too long after that she applied to the University of Pennsylvania for a master's in higher-education administration. Once back in a structure where she could clearly see the brass rings, she was the star again. She performed so well at Penn that the university made the unusual move of hiring her right out of its own program.

She was devoted to her job, admitting that much of her life circled around the campus. She even lived as a fellow in on-campus housing and was pursuing her Ph.D. on the side. Her hope was to build the sort of résumé that would allow her to become a dean of students someday or the president of a college.

Her urban tribe in Philadelphia was composed of about fifteen people with six members at its core, almost all of whom held jobs on campus. She was the coordinator of most of the group's activities, organizing frequent cocktail hours and group dinners at new restaurants and acting as coach for their summer softball team. They shared season tickets to Penn basketball and always seemed to be planning for the celebration of somebody's birthday.

Looking back on her time since starting her master's degree, Beth saw a clear positive progression in almost every aspect of her life. "Every year has gotten better," she said, not bragging but simply stating a fact. "I've become more secure financially and in my career. Every year I've felt more confident and happy."

The prospect of turning thirty didn't scare her in the least. Yet she had some lingering concerns about where she was in life as that milestone birthday approached. She could clearly remember how she imagined her future when she was twenty-one. At that younger age the idea of being thirty held the promise of progress on every front. Certainly, she remembers thinking, she would have managed to get married and start a family.

Beth knew that being single at thirty was not an aberration. Among her friends in Philadelphia, there were many in the same boat. However, there was another group of friends in her life who had taken a different route. Nearly all her friends from her Rosemont College days – good Catholic girls mostly – had tied the knot. The string of weddings (which she often attended in bridesmaid's gowns) had started in her early twenties and become a torrent in the last couple of years. In one sixteen-month period she attended sixteen weddings.

"I've begun to hate weddings," she said to me. This was a bit of a surprising admission, because Beth didn't seem like the kind of person to hate anything. "I sit at the back of the reception hall with the other college friends and I say to myself, 'Here comes the lousy dance music.'" Her willingness to dance joyfully to "Celebrate good times, come on!" had been sorely challenged.

The torrent of weddings of those college friends had recently let up for the simple reason that there were no more to get married. At the last wedding shower she attended, besides the bride-to-be, she was the only single woman. "At one point, I got everyone's attention and told them: 'Hey, if any one of you secretly feels sorry for me, please stop it. I feel fine. I'm happy doing what I'm doing. Really, I'm happy.'"

Judging by her good-natured demeanor, I certainly believed her. She knew she had a privileged life and a good job in an interesting city. She was devoted to the students she counseled, to her friends, and to her family back in New Jersey, which included two young nephews. She celebrated Christmas, Thanksgiving, and Easter with her blood family and spent Fourth of July, New Year's Eve, and Labor Day with her Philadelphia friends. She was sincerely grateful for it all.

But still, she wondered, what had happened in the marriage department? Her years of being single had yielded only a handful of short-term boyfriends. None of these relationships had even come close to ending in marriage. It frustrated her that she didn't exactly know why things had played out this way. As I talked with her, I became certain that a couple of reasons were *not* part of the answer.

For one, she had not hidden herself from the opportunity to meet men. Despite all the time she devoted to her job, her position as an administrator at a world-renowned university ensured that she was meeting a fairly constant stream of new, smart people. Besides, she wasn't one of those people who let work eclipse her social life. She played sports, ran charity races, and went out with friends frequently.

I was also sure that Beth had not adopted some *Sex in the City* lifestyle. She had not replaced the search for Mr. Right with a string of Mr. Right Nows. She had watched friends meet guys and quickly fall into physically intimate relationships, and she was uncomfortable that there didn't seem to be any middle gears in the dating world today. Beth thought that she might do better in a world where there was a little more structure to the courtship ritual, where you could go out on a date with someone without having to worry about sex right away.

So why had marriage been so elusive? It was probably true that the type of guy who would interest Beth would not come along every day. Certainly she would want a mate who matched her maturity and smarts and possessed the same sort of confidence and social acumen. I believed Beth had the talent and personality to realize her dream of heading up a college someday, and I saw no reason she shouldn't expect an equally promising man to be her mate. I knew, however, that men like that existed. I saw no reason why Beth should not have found one.

There was something about the way Beth was describing her dating life that reminded me of how she described her life right after college, when she was at a loss for what to do. An achiever by nature, Beth was willing to put in the effort toward finding a mate. The problem was that there didn't seem to be any steps to follow. When I suggested this to Beth, she agreed.

"It's true, it seems like all the rules for dating and for how to approach marriage are in flux," she said. "I think when I don't have a sense of rules or structure, I get confused. I like to think of myself as spontaneous, but I know I do better in situations where I know what's expected."

Beth had not intentionally turned her back on the institution of marriage. She did not, in Buchanan's words, need to be part of a "mass reconversion" to the notion that marriage and childbirth held the possibility for happiness. Quite the contrary, she saw great value and meaning in the institution. When she took the Myers Briggs test, her personality came up as a "traditionalist." She grew up a strong Catholic, baby-sitting constantly, and marriage and family had always felt like her birthright.

Many of the women I met who were part of the marriage delay had not intentionally pursued some alternative lifestyle – quite the opposite. Like Beth, they had a deep reverence and desire for marriage, but struggled in a dating world that made it unclear how to proceed. This seemed to me something the cultural commentators were missing. In placing blame, it was easier to vilify these women for having made choices rather than to understand the subtle and complex confluence of currents that had drifted them away from marriage and husbands.

The Advice Avalanche

People in Beth's uncertain position were the cause of a boomlet in publishing at the end of the nineties and into the new millennium. Thousands of magazine articles and dozens of advice books came out purporting to explain how women could overcome the confusion in the dating world and marry the man of their dreams. The people who wrote *The Rules*, *The Real Rules*, and *I Kissed Dating Goodbye* probably thought they were leading the cultural debate on the topic of sex and dating. The popularity of these advice books was an expression of just how thirsty we were as a population for someone to explain what was going on with the marriage delay.

The Rules, which recommends that women game men into loving and marrying them, was the most popular by far. *Rules* authors Ellen Fein and Sherrie Schneider advise women to adopt rules of courtship from a generation ago and make dating into an obstacle course for men. Men like games and challenges, was their thinking.

Notably, they did not lobby for a return to a no-sex-before-marriage policy or even to modesty. ("Hike up your skirt to entice the opposite sex!" they told readers, although they did not indicate to what height.) Rather, they told women to protect a kind of emotional virginity. This meant that having sex on the kitchen table was okay as long as the woman didn't let on that it meant she cared for the guy. "First and foremost, stay emotionally cool no matter how hot the sex gets," they counseled women when the book came out in 1995. And in the morning, "go quietly about your business – brush your teeth, do some sit-ups and stretches, brew coffee . . ." Most of all, remember to remain "casual and unmoved."

The Rules was not alone in wishing for a return to more traditional modes of courtship. The Christian best-seller *I Kissed Dating Goodbye* came out a year after *The Rules*. It argued that modern dating should be abandoned altogether in favor of scenarios in which a couple might exchange glances across the room during Bible study. Then there was *The Code: Time-Tested Secrets for Getting What You Want from Women Without Marrying Them!*, which claimed to reveal a secret set of rules by which men could avoid commitment and best embrace their true calling of being sexual opportunists. *The Code* encouraged men to "just say no to marriage."

These books (particularly *The Code* and *The Rules*) were played against each other in the popular press. Magazine writers and essayists assumed that within them, they were viewing a range of opinions about modern mating. But the range was narrower than it appeared. While the authors differed on the question of how to behave, they all agreed that modern dating had fallen apart to the extent that we needed their carefully packaged advice. *The Rules* bemoaned the belief that social paths of courtship had washed away, while *The Code* (agreeing that roads were out) encouraged men to do some manly off-roading.

I do remember that among my group of friends in San Francisco, there was a fair amount of talk about these books, as there was about all things that had to do with mating, but I don't remember much deep interest. We talked about the authors the way one might have talked about traveling nostrum sellers who were pitching cure-alls to a gullible population. The daring of these writers intrigued us – their near-religious devotion to obviously bland cure-alls and their blindness to their inevitable public humiliation.* That their ideas seemed to be popular for a time was hard to get upset about. Most of our interest came from knowing that the readers would eventually discover that the potions didn't work.

While the cures offered by these advice-book authors were nothing more than mixtures of conventional wisdom, the problem they were trying to address seemed real enough to many women. Other, more convincing voices agreed that a decline of social controls and expectations for romantic relationship had left an entire generation wandering lost through our young adulthood.

For instance, a social psychologist named Leon Kass wrote a paper titled "The End of Courtship," in which he observed that my generation was doomed. "Things were not always like this, in fact, one suspects things were never like this, not here, not anywhere," Kass wrote in classic everything-is-going-to-hell tones. The whole system of romance, he argued, from first glance to marriage, had broken down. In his words, there were "no socially prescribed forms of conduct to help guide young men and women in the direction of matrimony." This had led us to become "sexually hyperactive . . . all at once casual and carefree and grim and humorless about getting along with the opposite sex."

Kass pointed to our early socialization as one reason for this sad behavior. We were a generation who had suffered the "psychic and moral maiming" of the high divorce rates of our parents' generation. Having grown up in the lap of luxury, we were "spoiled children" interested only in our short-term self-interest.

Beyond that, however, it was women whom he believed responsible for the evaporation of courtship and for the rude, loveless rutting that

---

* Coauthor Ellen Fein was forced to announce her divorce from her middle-aged pharmacist husband just prior to the publication for *Rules III: Time-Tested Secrets for Making Your Marriage Work.* The spin Fein tried to put on this turn of events proved what a huckster she was. "I was very happily married for many, many years before the [first *Rules*] book came out," she wrote in an online chat session. "The sudden rise to fame was just too much for me. I had stopped going out on date night and was too tired to do all the things I used to do . . . Rather than filing for divorce, a few weekends away alone would have been better!"

had come to replace it. In times past, he reminded us, the supreme virtue of a woman was modesty, that is, "sexual self-control, manifested not only in chastity but in decorous dress and manner, speech and deed, and in reticence in the display of her well-banked affections."

"A fine woman understood that giving her body meant giving her heart," he wrote, "which was too precious to be bestowed on anyone who would not prove himself worthy, *at the very least* by pledging himself in marriage to be her defender and lover forever" [italics *mine*].

The worst result of women having become slutty, Kass argued, was that this behavior kept men from being able to fall in love and marry them. As he explained: "Once female modesty became the first casualty of the sexual revolution, even women eager for marriage lost their greatest power to hold and to discipline their prospective mates. For it is woman's refusal of sexual importunings, coupled with hints or promises of later gratification, that is generally a necessary condition of transforming a man's lust into love . . . Why would a man court a woman for marriage when she may be sexually enjoyed, and regularly, without it?"

Why indeed? Why would a man give 100 percent devotion when he was getting laid with a less taxing 51 percent? Apparently, men were just doing the math that their natural-born maleness required them to do.

That women were giving it away was bad for everyone, especially women. "For the first time in human history," wrote Kass, "mature women by the tens of thousands live the entire decade of their twenties – their most fertile years – neither in the homes of their fathers nor in the homes of their husbands; unprotected, lonely, and out of sync with their inborn nature."

Kass was kind enough to offer pity, of a sort, to the poor people writhing in the purgatory of modern dating. Speaking on behalf of his generation, Kass wrote: "Our hearts go out . . . to the lonely, disappointed, cynical, misguided or despondent people who are missing out on one of life's greatest adventures [that is, traditional

171

courtship and marriage] and, through it, on many of life's deepest experiences, insights, and joys. We watch our sons and daughters, our friends' children, and our students bumble along from one unsatisfactory relationship to the next, wishing we could help . . . [in these] melancholy times."

Hooking Up

There was some empirical evidence for Kass's conclusions. Sociologists Norval Glenn and Elizabeth Marquardt issued an attention-grabbing report on the sexual habits of young college women. Titled "Hooking Up, Hanging Out, and Hoping for Mr. Right," the results made all the papers, for it was a remarkably readable – at times almost spicy – glimpse into how young college women were going about their love lives.

The researchers and the popular press tended to focus on the data in the paper that pointed to the breakdown of courtship. Notably, the study gave public life to the term "hooking up," which three out of four women in the survey defined as "when a girl and a guy get together for a physical encounter and don't necessarily expect anything further." The term was apparently ambiguous about how physical the "physical encounter" would get. "Hooking up" could mean anything from smooching on down.

Women also described the practice of "hanging out," which had purportedly replaced formal dating. Hanging out was when "women and men spent loosely organized, undefined time together," according to the study. "Women or men could invite each other to come over to their dorm or apartment and hang out to watch a movie, alone or among friends, or they might hang out together at the library and study." Hanging out could lead to some hooking up, which might or might not lead to an ongoing romantic relationship.

Viewed against the dating styles of the 1950s, these new practices did sound pretty unromantic. Where were the fraternity pins, the corsages, and the formal dances? Overall, the researchers concluded, there had been a disappearance of traditional courtship on college campuses. The social norms and expectations that once helped young people find a pathway to marriage had up and vanished.

"Because social processes for mating and dating are not clear," the report concluded, "these college women often feel they must make up their own rules as they go along . . . Many of these women are clearly trying to sort out their next steps largely alone."

In the popular press, the report was greeted with the usual cries that everything was changing for the worse. Political commentators love studies like this one, because they get to express their outrage while titillating their audience at the same time. The practice of "hooking up" got the most ink. The idea that college women were giving it away at the drop of hat, not even expecting a ride home in return, spawned many arousing diatribes from conservative pundits.

Was Courtship as Dead as These Obituaries Maintained?

Time and again, in reading about my generation, I had come across what I called "the siren songs of the old." The chorus went something like: "Everything has changed since I was young / Oh, how much worse things have become!"

With courtship it was clear that things *had* changed quickly, but there was significant evidence that the change had been one of style more than substance. Take, for instance, some seldom-mentioned statistics in the hooking-up survey. It turned out that while most all college women knew what "hooking up" meant, few women actually hooked up on a regular basis. Fully 60 percent of women surveyed reported that they themselves had never hooked up. And while that left a substantial 40 percent who had, only 10 percent of those surveyed said they had hooked up more than six times. Everyone seemed to be convinced that hooking up happened often or fairly often, but it appeared that they were always talking about someone besides themselves. When it came to the ubiquity of hooking up, there was a lot more talk than tango. Despite what one might have surmised from the popular press, the practice had not become the norm for sexual activity on campuses.

173

Neither was it true that traditional dating had entirely disappeared from campuses. Many more women reported going on traditional dates, in fact, than reported "hooking up." Regular old boyfriend-girlfriend bonds were common, as were intense "joined-at-the-hip" relationships. Almost half of the women surveyed reported having a boyfriend, and 24 percent of those said they had never had sex. Courtship terms might have changed, but love, devotion, and chastity were still in play.

Marriage was also very much on the minds of these modern coeds. Over half of all college women surveyed reported that they would like to meet their future husbands in college. Nearly all said that being married someday was a "very important" goal and that they understood that "the things I do in my relationship today will affect my future marriage."

There were other statistics from the "Hooking Up, Hanging Out" survey that contradicted the general impression that everything was turning bleak and sleazy for young women and romance. Fully 88 percent reported being happy with the social scenes at their colleges. Sixty-four percent felt sex without commitment was wrong. And nearly all women – 96 percent, in fact – felt they had a clear sense of what they should and should not do in romantic/sexual interactions.

From certain perspectives, things weren't going terribly wrong; they were going terribly right.

Hidden Agendas

Rereading Buchanan and Kass, I came to believe that their main mistake was in attempting to discretely parse out courtship from the massive social movements that have influenced its change. Perhaps this was a strategic move. By choosing to focus on courtship, social critics could curse the fact that young men no longer sat on front porches, hats on their laps, being interrogated as to their worthiness by stern fathers and protective mothers. It was hard to argue against

174

this vision of a time when dating was not a roller coaster but a progression as steady and predictable as a Ferris wheel.

But this kind of selective nostalgia was bad – perhaps even dangerous – social science. I became as skeptical of those who longed for old-fashioned courtship as I was of those who fondly remember how German fascists got the trains to run on time. In their nostalgia they had failed to fully remember the sexism and racism inherent in courtship rituals of old.

Not that blatant sexism didn't sometimes slip into their arguments. Kass's question "Why would a man court a woman for marriage when she may be sexually enjoyed, and regularly, without it?" was a dead giveaway. It seems to me that anyone who would ask such a rhetorical question doesn't think much of women. The question clearly implies that the primary value of a woman's companionship comes from her neck-down attributes.

Equally ridiculous is the idea that a man can't fall in love unless the woman he's dating withholds sex. Underlying this idea is the hilarious notion that sexual frustration brings on the clarity of thought with which one would want to make a life-altering commitment. The truth couldn't be more the reverse: Unsatisfied sexual desire is the sand to the engine of the mind. The most foolish decisions a man will make in his life will be done under the influence of sexual longing. ("I'll shoot the president and then Jodie Foster will notice me," was John Hinckley's logic. He was an aberration, I might add, only in his actions, not in the fact that he thought of something so ludicrous.) Would we really want the decision to get married to be one of them? Good God, no. A man possessed by sexual desire can't be counted on to change lanes safely, much less his life's course.

This was equally true from the woman's perspective. How could a woman be sure of the kind of man she was marrying if she had leveraged the half nelson of short-term desire into a long-term commitment? The woman who withholds sex from a romantic partner to get the guy to jump through hoops like a dog doesn't really know the man. The women of my generation knew that the most meaningful test of a man's interest was how he treated her after they had sex. After climax, does he slink away mumbling something about having a lot of work to do? Does he get up and make an omelet? Or does he remain attentive and say something so sweet and charming that the woman's heart pounds for the meaningfulness of the moment? This was not to suggest that women of my generation deliberately used sex as a test, but they were savvy enough to know that what a man did *after* getting into the sack was a far better indicator of his intentions than what he would do to get there.

In longing for the bygone day when courtship was king, social pundits were selectively remembering the rosy aspects from a time when marriages were often entered into for practical and unromantic reasons. Describing the days when courtship guided behavior Kass even admitted that "most of us stepped forward into married life . . . without much pondering. We were simply doing what our parents had done." My generation was clearly not taking this sort of somnambulant approach to the altar, and I, for one, was not sad about that fact.

Kass, Buchanan, and others were right about women being the reason for most of the change in courtship, but they got the particulars wrong. In a 1965 survey, fully three out of four college women said they'd marry a man they didn't love if he fit their criteria in every other way, while the men of that time insisted that they wanted to marry for love. What had changed in thirty-five years was that women now expected to marry for love also. The difference between previous generations and mine was not that we devalued courtship and marriage but that we had dramatically raised its stakes. Women in my time were flabbergasted by the idea that a woman would even consider marrying a man who "fit their criteria." Ninety percent of women and men alike now wanted to marry their soul mates. We had become more idealistic about marriage – we were holding the marriage union to a higher standard than any generation before us.

Once it got around that our first criterion in marriage was finding a soul mate, a new set of social commentators came on the scene to chastise us for being too romantic. These new critics worried that our lofty expectations would keep us from marrying and, if we married, lead us to quick divorces. They wanted to warn us that marriages were hard work. Iris Krasnow warned in her book *Surrendering to Marriage*, "Here's the straight truth: A) Marriage can be hell. B) The grass is not greener on the other side. C) Nobody is perfect – including you. D) So you may as well love the one you are with."

But looking for a soul mate to marry did not necessarily mean that we harbored some fragile set of sensibilities that were doomed to be shattered. We might have been idealistic about marriage, but we were hardened realists about relationships. Most of us had had multiple-year girlfriends or boyfriends, and many had lived with one or more romantic partners. I was quite sure that we were much savvier than our parents were about the Sturm und Drang inherent in any long-term partnerships. In short, we were idealistic in thought and intention while we were hardened and realistic from experience – which is, if you think about it, a pretty fine way to take on any complex life project.

What Women Did While They Waited

In the end, whether you saw the marriage delay as disastrous for women and their chances to make happy partnerships depended on how you valued the things they accomplished with their lives during the delay. Take a woman like Beth. She had been extremely busy during her twenties. She had filled this time with education, career success, and loyal friendships. She was far from the exception.

Women weren't just treading water during their single years. Sixty percent of all single women owned their own homes (snapping them up much faster than single men did). Hundreds of travel companies had become savvy to this population's thirst for adventure, offering increasingly challenging women-only treks across deserts and over mountains. Their advance into careers once dominated by men was remarkably swift – every bit as important as the mold-breaking their mothers managed. The statistics, and pretty much all of the anecdotal evidence I found, pointed to the conclusion that these women were becoming remarkably self-sufficient and confident adults.

When my mother came and visited my tribe of friends in San Francisco, the women would consistently amaze her. After each dinner party or Thanksgiving celebration, she couldn't stop talking about these successful and confident women. As a feminist herself, she was giddy with pride for their careers in law, medicine, and business, but there was something more. She was impressed not just by their résumés but with how remarkably competent they seemed in every aspect of their lives. This is not to say that she didn't like my male friends – she did – but there was a clear difference. The men in my tribe might have been successful in one or another endeavor, but in general we did not tackle life nearly as aggressively as the women did.

"The women I've talked to are extremely competent at a great many things," said Barbara Dafoe Whitehead, a researcher who has devoted the last few years to studying young unmarried women. "Women can manage friendships, work lives, exciting travel. Men have a hard time with that kind of range."

So why were marriage and family such a constant worry for many women in terms of achieving their life goals? I came to believe that women's anxieties about marriage came not from the disappearance of courtship but because we were a generation living through a massive transition in the very nature and meaning of being a young adult. What will seem weird to future generations is that we lived during the brief moment in history when we perceived the personal and professional accomplishments of women as being in conflict with their hopes of finding happy marriages. Once we're out of this nervous transition period, it will seem bizarre that we failed to make a causal connection between a woman's general success in her single years and her potential for a happy marriage.

For men, societies have long assumed that their solo accomplishments made them more valuable as mates. That was why we were usually expected to marry later than women, providing us with time not simply to achieve material success but also to mature into confident, full-fledged men. When such a man entered a relationship, we rightly had more hope for its outcome. We saw the achievements of his single years as *directly connected* to his value and potential as a mate.

My bet was that the next generation would make this same assumption for women as well. But the fact that my generation of women did not yet have this cultural narrative in place did not mean that they would not reap the same benefits. The sociologists I talked to all agreed that the vast majority of the never-married women would eventually marry. I had no doubt that for a woman like Beth, when she did marry, the emotional growth and accomplishments of her single twenties would make the odds of that marriage's survival remarkably good.

It's understandable that a generation extending its single years to unheard-of lengths might become nervous. Single people tended to see themselves as a failure in the marriage game until they found themselves in a relationship headed for the altar. They perceived little gray area in their love lives – things were either going great or badly. From the standpoint of being single, it was hard to see the connection between one's individual growth and the success of an imagined future marriage.

But if it was true, as I believed, that women (and men) were preparing themselves for healthy marriages even as they flew solo, it would certainly affect the course of true love when it came along. In particular, such maturing would affect the length of time it took us to marry once we found the right person. In short, we would be more ready than a twenty-two-year-old would when that right person arrived. I had only anecdotal evidence, but I was convinced that when we were lucky enough to fall in love, the course toward marriage would be measured in months, not years.

There was also reason to hope that these eventual marriages would be happier and last longer. It made sense, after all, that a marriage forged by confident, full-fledged men and women would be stronger than those formed between two people still struggling to become adults.

The early statistics on the success of my generation's marriages seemed to bolster this conclusion. While reading statistical papers on marriage one day, I was happy to learn that the divorce rate had recently begun to decline after a generation of steadily increasing. What was behind this remarkable sea change? Tim Heaton, a researcher at the Department of Sociology at Brigham Young University, discerned that the more successful marriages were those that started later between couples with higher levels of education. Apparently, despite all the doom and gloom about the marriage delay, when we finally did get married, our marriages were tending to last longer.

A Nerve-Racking Transition Coming to a Close

If the vast majority of never-marrieds eventually forge strong marriages, the next generation of women who delay will likely not be haunted by the possibility that their delay means they are doomed to a life alone. They will understand that the maturing they do on their own will reap benefits in their eventual marriages. They will also likely be less afraid of all the news about infertility in their thirties as they watch the cohort ahead of them hatch babies by the millions. While much has been made of the post-thirty drop in fertility rates among women, the numbers, to my eyes, aren't that scary. Fully two out of three women thirty-five to thirty-nine can get pregnant *within a year*. For a couple in their late thirties that tries for two years, the odds rise to 91 percent. If you are not overweight or underweight and treat your body relatively well, your chances go up from there.

Already there was evidence that the confusion and fear were lifting. Not too long after I talked with Beth, I met Patty, who had recently graduated from UCLA. Twenty-three, she had a square-shouldered, straightforward demeanor that made her seem older. Recently she had been working hard on her law-school applications. The weekend before we talked she had completed her LSAT test, and she worried that she might have frozen up on the first section. She wasn't upset; her future looked bright regardless. If she choked, she'd just take the exam again. If she doesn't get into law school this year, there's always the next.

The only thing that had upset her lately was the fact that in a two-week period, as she was studying for the LSATs, no fewer than five of her friends from college had announced their engagements. "I was shocked and mildly disturbed by these early marriages," she told me. "I always thought my friends would marry in their late twenties or early thirties. I thought that this time of life after college was for self-exploration and becoming a person on one's own."

When I asked her what she imagined for her twenties, she mapped it out. From twenty-four to twenty-seven she would be in law school, and she hoped to pass the bar exam at twenty-eight. That left her the next few years to start her career, date, and fall in love with someone she wanted to marry. She hoped to have started a family by the time she was thirty-five.

She wondered whether her friends who had recently gotten engaged had done so out of a reaction to the frightening transition from college to the real world.

"I don't want to be married now," she said plainly. "I am going to law school and building a life for myself."

She doesn't have everything worked out. Patty knows that her plan to find Mr. Right between the ages of twenty-eight and thirty requires more than a bit of luck that he'll actually show up on the scene. She has also seen how older working women with professional careers have given over much of the child rearing to nannies and day care centers. She didn't like the looks of that sort of mothering, but she didn't yet know how she would balance work and family.

She was not dismissing marriage because it would get in the way of her career; rather, she felt she needed to make personal strides before making such a life change. She saw meaning and value in such a progression to marriage. This is not to say that life will be easy for Patty or that everything will come off on schedule. There will be meaningful differences, however, in how young women like Patty think about their lives compared to those who forged the marriage

181

delay. If Patty approaches her thirtieth birthday and is still single, for instance, it will not be a mystery as to how she got there. That outcome was part of the plan.

One Down, Forty-Three Million to Go

I remember the odd moment when my friend Jennifer showed me her engagement ring. There it was, a monster ruby bordered on two sides by four slender baguette diamonds in a platinum setting. Just this act, Jennifer holding out her left hand, chin high, wrist cocked downward, for me to ooh and ah, seemed like a fifties period piece. The gesture was so very un-Jennifer.

If she hadn't been so obviously proud and I hadn't been so legitimately impressed by the ring and happy for her, we would no doubt have ironically deconstructed the moment. I would have pointed out that in displaying her ring, she was acting like the sort of unsophisticated big-haired Jersey girl that she moved to San Francisco to avoid becoming. She would have played the part, putting on a working-class Jersey accent and making up something about her fiancé's Corvette. But this didn't happen. We were pointedly nonironic.

As I did with many women of my generation, I had always wondered about Jennifer's feelings about marriage. Over the years, when I asked her if she hoped to get married, she would never give me a straight answer. Sometimes she espoused the hard-line feminist ideology that marriage was a type of legal prostitution or enslavement of women, but I never really believed this reflected her true feelings. Being a smart and fast-talking lawyer, she could argue multiple sides of any issue and often did so just to befuddle you.

Her personal ambivalence about marriage was more complex than that. How she felt about marriage seemed to have most to do with how she felt about the individual union at hand. If a friend married the wrong guy, she'd get angry at the friend and at the institution of marriage all at once. She wept so copiously at one friend's wedding that she fell off her chair, sobbing like the mothers of martyred sons do on the TV news. In this case she saw the institution of marriage as part of the problem. Marriage was the mechanism for the downfall of her friend.

To my eyes, her personal feelings about marriage did not change over time; rather they seemed to well up through a confluence of her life's events. Through one of the weak ties in our group she started to date a smart and funny journalist for *Newsweek* magazine. Within a year or so they had moved in together and adopted a cat that they talked about incessantly. (When the rules of courtship for our generation are written, the adopting of a cat will be a clear signal of impending nuptials.) When Brad proposed, no one was surprised that Jen said yes.

I know that Jen felt no regrets about her single years. It was a remarkable string of successes. She had opened her own law office, where she focused on free-speech rights, and then was hired at Stanford to run the legal clinic for the law school. She had been instrumental in holding our tribe of people together by being a constant organizer of events and a counselor to whoever was feeling low. She did not even regret the failed relationships she went through. Looking back, it all seemed important: the inevitable course to the person she had become. She was thirty-three when she married. She hadn't gotten married late. She had married right on time.

Chapter 8

LOVE VERSUS THE TRIBE

You might assume that life in the urban tribe would be compatible with, even complementary to, the quest of finding love in the city. Some single people I talked to did attest that their tribes were helpful in the search for true love. Through friends-of-friends networks, for instance, many people told me, tribe membership provided them with a relatively safe way to meet more potential boyfriends or girlfriends than they would have been able to come across on their own. In an active tribe, there was always someone who knew of a party or was willing to go out on the town together looking for love. Others were thankful that having an active social life within the tribe took the pressure off the need to have a boyfriend or girlfriend. Because they had friends, they said, they were less likely to date a marginal prospect for fear of being lonely.

"This tribe has made me realize that I can be happy living my life my way," wrote Kari, twenty-six, from Pittsburgh. "My tribe will not let me waste time on a loser." In very similar language, Rebecca, also twenty-six, from Dallas wrote, "The group has helped my romantic life because it has strengthened my self-esteem. I will not settle for anything less than true love and passion with complete respect. If it hadn't been for the tribe I may have married the wrong person for the wrong reasons."

Similarly, tribe members also attested that they had learned through the tribe what they were looking for in a mate. When people told me they were still looking for their soul mates, I often asked them to define the term. I had the suspicion that no one actually knew what "soul mate" meant. Very often, however, people told me that they had come to understand the characteristics of a "soul mate" through their relationships with their friends. "Our tribe exists out of our deep desire to be with others whose souls match with ours," wrote Maschelle from Charleston about her all-female group. "We are soul mates without sex. As we search for soul mates *with* sex we find great comfort in each other."

Similarly, Frieda in Oakland reported that the qualities of the men in her tribe raised the bar for what she was looking for in a boyfriend. "I want to meet a man with a combination of the qualities of the men in my posse." Why didn't she just date those men she admired? She couldn't do that, she wrote, "because that would be like sleeping with family."

For many of us in tribes, walking into a roomful of friends brought with it a level of emotional ease that set the rest of city life in relief. Through our friendships, we had learned what it felt like to be comfortable in our own skin and learned to be suspicious of other relationships where we didn't feel a similar peace. *Washington Post* columnist Jeanne Marie Laskas saw that the possibility for humiliation existed in every aspect of her life except one: her tribe of friends she called "the Babes." Within that context, she felt no expectation that she had to be constantly smart or attractive or "on." In fact, when she was around her friends, she felt she didn't have to do anything at all. "I don't have to participate," she writes. "No one is going to judge me if I just sit here daydreaming. That's what the Babes are all about. The freedom to just be." In this way, tribes informed us of the ultimate goal for our romantic lives: a partner who allowed us to feel as safe and true to ourselves as we felt when we were around our friends. We had become familiar with a particular type of consistent love and support that we would be unwilling to live without.

While this might seem like yet another positive attribute of the tribe, it brought with it a problem. As exciting as new lovers could be, they seldom compared with our tribes in terms of comfort level. Our romantic relationships, by their nature, were more risky, and they required a type of directed attention and emotional energy that was rarely necessary in long-established friendships. I could see that difference when friends would sometimes meet up with the group, late in the evening, after going out on a first or second date. Regardless of how well the date went, these friends looked like they had just finished a job interview. Once they were with the group, I could see the weight come off their shoulders. Their jaws would relax from the effort of constantly smiling. The women would take off their stylish but uncomfortable shoes.

The fact that it was unfair to compare a new love with old friends did not stop people from doing so. Maschelle, for instance, who described her friends as soul mates without sex, wrote that she and her friends often doubted whether it was possible to find a similarly deep and effortless connection with a romantic partner. "I haven't met a man who has fulfilled me emotionally as much as my girls have," Sandy from Manhattan told me similarly. "Because I'm so happy with them, a guy would really have a tough role to fill if he were to come into my life for good – you can't have your tribe and husband too – it's a tall order to fill."

I suspected the truth was that no romantic relationship was ever going to be as uniquely comfortable as our friendships. This was certainly true during the high-pressure beginnings of a romance, but I wondered whether it was true in the long run as well. Might friendships always be the safe bet compared with the high-stakes gamble of investing in a single relationship? One of the things that made friendships so relaxed was that they did not require constant attention. Serious romantic relationships, at least as I had experienced them up to that point in my life, needed daily maintenance lest the roller coaster fly off the track.

For those who lived ten or fifteen years within a tribe, the contrast between the emotional safety of friendships and the tribulations of romance became only more pronounced. After surviving a number of romantic disasters, friendships could seem like the only dependable relationships around. Some tribe members told me that after several failed romances, they began to put their tribes ahead of their dating lives. This was sometimes a conscious decision, as it was for thirty-one-year-old Marjolein of Rotterdam, Holland, who felt so satisfied with her social life that she wrote, "Quite frankly, I'm no longer looking for a date or partner or whatever."

In other cases, tribal life seemed to slowly edge out the romantic lives of the members without the members having made a conscious choice about it. "Being part of this tribe has impacted my love life significantly," wrote Andrea from San Diego. "I date far less now than I did previously. My free hours are spent occupied happily in the company of people who I respect and enjoy. I no longer do the single 'going out to meet someone.'"

Half of Kevin's ten-person tribe in Philadelphia was engaged to be married before the group formed. While he didn't draw a direct causal connection between the breaking off of those engagements with the creation of the group, he did see a clear connection between tribe membership and the fact that none of them subsequently found partners to marry. "Ultimately we all have the desire to be married," wrote Kevin. "We realize membership in this unique group creates a problem with maintaining romantic relationships outside of the group. I've been torn at times between an impulse to break away from these people and maintaining the comfort they bring to my life."

"My tribe was a large contributor to the failure of my last relationship," wrote Lisa, thirty-three, from New York. "My boyfriend felt that although we were together all the time, we didn't get enough 'alone time,' and he felt he was always having to compete for my attention."

The collective strength of tribal friendships could also impact individuals' ability or inclination to take a romantic relationship from one level to the next. "When I didn't have a boyfriend it was easy not to worry about dating because I was so busy with fun group activities and so fulfilled by my male and female friendships," wrote Deborah, twenty-six, from Columbus. "I now have a boyfriend, but if things don't work out I think that I could always find friends to support me and share my life with. I'm not going to get married just to get married, because life in a tribe is not lonely."

In these ways tribal life often gained a momentum that led members away from seeking out or focusing on relationships that might lead to marriage. Given that the vast majority of yet-to-be marrieds expressed a deep desire to one day find an appropriate spouse and have a family, I worried whether life in the tribe might have been inadvertently leading people away from this goal.

I certainly worried about this for myself. As I spent more time in the easy company of my friends, I worried that I would never have the courage to take the leap of faith a truly committed relationship would require. As I've described, tribes usually provided support and encouragement for taking risks. I was beginning to realize, however, that romance might be the one *monumental* exception to this truth. The consistent emotional safe haven that tribes provided allowed some, myself included, to avoid taking risks in their love lives.

"I have not had a romantic life for the eight and a half years I've been part of this tribe," wrote Jennifer, thirty-one, from Chicago. "I wonder sometimes if I used this tribe to escape the romantic life to avoid what I feared most: rejection and/or being left."

Queen Bees and Cockblockers

Of course urban tribes were not opposed to their members finding happy romances. Tribes, in fact, were usually made up of a mixture of singles and couples. Serious relationships that were formed within the group or existed prior to the tribe often became central to the group's dynamics. Certain couples became quasiparental figures to the singles in the tribe.

For perpetually single members, however, there was friction. They pointed out dozens of ways they felt that their tribes were sabotaging their dating lives. In the competition for mates, for example, male "cockblockers" in tribes could create a kind of force field around the group that repelled available women. Charles in Denver noticed that one member of his group, I'll call him Darren, would throw himself at every new attractive girl who came within the tribe's vicinity. Although Darren was almost never successful, the result was that he scared new women from coming to group functions. Darren was a classic cock-blocker – i.e., a male who, through futile sexual importuning of every woman in sight, ruined the romantic chances of the coyer males.

Queen bees in tribes could be problematic as well. A queen bee was usually an attractive and charming woman in the tribe, who preferred that all flirtatious energy be directed toward her. For the men, the effect of the queen bee depended on the circumstances. For a single man, a queen bee was great to have in the tribe, as she could be guaranteed to give you gobs of attention and affection (although usually not of the overtly sexual variety). However, if a male in the tribe was to bring a new love interest around, the queen bee could be counted on to find that woman lacking. No woman, a queen bee would attest, was good enough to date the men in her tribe. It was a nice sentiment, but her motivations were greedy: She wanted the attention for herself. For other women in the group, the queen bee could be the equivalent of the male cockblocker.

To complicate matters, within most coed tribes there existed a dense tangle of long-standing flirtations, unexpressed crushes, and glimmers of mutual attraction. While sometimes this sexual energy would find direct expression, when two people would hook up or start a romance, often it existed in the group as a kind of ambient sexual charge. It was common, for instance, for tribe members to share the same bed or tent on trips, skinny-dip, give each other massages, or sleep on each other's shoulders during long car rides. Looked at individually, these activities usually were clearly platonic – that is, they rarely crossed the line into overtly sexual play. However, it was obvious that they were not without their sexual component. Added together, they looked less innocent. For single people, tribes were a source of a goodly amount of sexual gratification.

It might be too strong to say that tribes became the equivalent of surrogate lovers. However, the flirtation combined with the physical touching combined with a deep emotional connection often put these groups in direct competition with our romances. For this reason, throwing a new romantic interest in with your group could be as suicidal as inviting your ex-girlfriend or ex-boyfriend along on a first date. The chances of everyone hitting it off and feeling at ease were, to put it mildly, not good.

The main point here was that for long-term single members, tribes created an emotional life that in its fullness and scope would inevitably conflict with the beginnings of a serious romance. One might have the emotional energy to date casually while in the tribe, but investing in a serious relationship usually required a choice of where one's loyalty lay. Everyone has had the feeling of losing a friend's attention when he or she got caught up in a fast-paced romance. The difference was that tribes had the collective power to lobby an individual not to leave. Indeed, when a new romance bloomed, a tribe could, as a group, react with the same sort of jealousy as a lover who was about to be left behind.

He's Not Right for You

Jill, thirty-one, was a happy member of a Boston tribe of artsy bohemians until she started dating Andrew, thirty-four, a successful young businessman who chaired a richly endowed grant foundation.*
Jill hadn't dated anyone in several years, and her friends initially said they were pleased to hear that she had a new romance. Jill was excited to introduce Andrew to the group, and on their fourth date she brought him to a tribe gathering, which happened to be a party for Bill's thirtieth birthday.

His appearance at the party made clear that there was an obvious culture clash between Andrew and the rest of the group. Bill was a waiter who aspired to be painter. He held the party in his warehouse/studio at the edge of town. Although Andrew's foundation gave grants

* I've changed the names and some identifying details for this story.

to artists and filmmakers, Andrew himself dressed and acted more like an investment banker. He hadn't changed clothes from work, and he stuck out in his Armani suit. But it wasn't just his clothes that group members found off-putting. He had an upper-crust Bostonian accent that many in Jill's tribe found curious when they learned he had grown up in New Jersey. He showed no deference to the other men in the group, often taking over conversations, giving his opinion on everything from international politics to postmodern literature. At one point he made a derogatory comment about one of Bill's paintings without realizing that he was talking to one of Bill's close friends.

The initial assessment of the women in the group was damning. To their eyes he was clearly untrustworthy. At the party he was seen appearing to flirt with a young gallery assistant for over half an hour. Casey, a central member of the tribe, even believed that Andrew had come on to her (although she was known to be something of a flirt herself). The women also noticed that Andrew gave inadequate attention to Jill, leaving her side for much of the night, and when he was with her he appeared unsolicitous.

Tribes love nothing more than to talk about the love lives of their members, and for days after Bill's birthday party there were dozens of conversations and one-to-one e-mail exchanges evaluating the new romance. The consensus was clear: Nobody liked Andrew. Even those who had not talked to him or who had missed the party altogether were convinced through the stories others passed around that he was bad news. Initially, Jill heard none of this. No one felt the need to warn Jill away, because they all assumed that it wouldn't be long until Jill came to her senses and dumped him. To their surprise, however, the relationship continued. When Jill showed up at group events, Andrew was inevitably at her side.

In certain social circles Boston is a small town, and it was not long until a story about Andrew drifted into the tribe's orbit. A tribe member named Diane knew a college friend of Andrew's, who reported that Andrew had recently been forced to change companies after he was caught simultaneously dating two women in his firm.

Worse yet, there were rumors that one of those relationships was ongoing. Diane was given the unpleasant job of passing the information on to Jill. To the group's surprise, Jill seemed unfazed. At first, she refused to believe the rumors; later, when a second source and then a third confirmed them, she made the case that Andrew had reformed.

In their own ways, others in the tribe began to reveal their feelings about Andrew. Jill didn't fail to notice that several of her friends avoided greeting or talking with Andrew at group events. Others made slyly derogatory remarks about the narrow-mindedness of art foundations, how they always supported the least interesting artists. Bill, for his part, began a new series of paintings of cavemen dressed in business attire. Everyone's favorite depicted a group of Neanderthals in Italian suits and red power ties gorging at the carcass of a gazelle.

On the group's first ski trip that year, Andrew's relations with the tribe only worsened. Andrew no doubt, understood on some level that he was not well liked. Instead of making an effort to win the group over, he simply tried to stay out of their way. An expert skier, he ditched Jill and the rest of the group and spent the days skiing the black diamond runs. The first night, at the cabin, he read a magazine as the rest of the group prepared dinner. Later, while everyone else played charades, Andrew stayed in the kitchen hunched over his laptop catching up on his e-mail. The second night he disappeared altogether to visit a nearby ski house that had been rented by friends he knew through work.

Over the next weeks, more and more members of the tribe made it clear to Jill what they thought of Andrew, although they often couched their opinion in concern for her. "He doesn't seem to treat you very nicely," they would say. "You deserve better."

When Jill continued to date Andrew, the tribe began to act collectively. Little by little the group built a consensus that no one wanted him invited to the group's New Year's Eve party. Jill was angry when Bill told her of the group's decision. Why was it any of their concern whom she dated? she wanted to know. Bill gave the party line: Andrew's treatment of Jill made everyone feel uncomfortable. The truth was also that nobody liked Andrew.

By excluding Andrew from such a key tribe function, the group had begun to communicate their ultimatum. Jill would be expected to choose between the group and her new boyfriend.

No One's Right for You

The dilemma Jill found herself in was far from an extreme case. The tribulations of having a new love approved by the group were, by far, the number-one negative story told to me about tribes.

Alissa, thirty-five, wrote that her tribe of sixteen in San Francisco practically ran her dating life. "When my tribe didn't like someone I dated, it greatly impacted that relationship," she told me. "I stopped dating one guy because he didn't fit well in my group."

Jen, twenty-four, from Chicago, also felt the force of this group influence. "I'm currently dating, and for the first time in a year and a half I'm truly happy, and it's almost as if my group is not happy for me," she wrote. "They ridicule me for not spending as much time with them, and that makes me feel guilty for being happy. They can say mean things to me about it, but I will try to resolve it with them even if it means ending my relationship. Friends will be there after a relationship ends, and I don't want to lose them. I depend on them so much that I can't imagine them not being in my life."

Kathy from San Francisco described an almost identical tension. "I now have a serious boyfriend, really for the first time since moving to San Francisco. My single friends are not happy because they don't have me as a single girl to go out with anymore. There is a sense of jealousy or a little bitterness by a couple girlfriends. A lot of the comments are about 'losing me,' or inferring that I don't want to go out with the girls just because I have a boyfriend."

Many tribe members were unabashed about the social pressure they used to influence the romantic choices of their friends. "Dating tagalongs are placed under severe scrutiny," wrote Ryan, twenty-six, from Denver, adding that the group informally votes on the acceptance of the new suitor into the group.

"I stopped talking to one of my girlfriends while she dated a guy I thought was a jerk," wrote Sandy from New York. She added that their friendship was patched up only after her friend's romance broke up. Membership in the tribe was often at stake. "People have rarely been kicked out of the group," Trina, twenty-nine, from Chicago wrote, "unless they crawl so far up their significant other's ass that they disappear."

Interestingly, many people didn't seem to mind the immense power their friends wielded in approving or disapproving of new romances; in fact, they imbued the tribes' opinions with great meaning. "I would never consider marrying anyone who was disliked by the tribe," wrote Sarah from Cedar Rapids. "It's an unspoken rule that nobody is allowed to marry unless we've met and liked that person. I think my friends are somewhat clairvoyant in being able to tell if someone is right or not."

"I think that I can trust the tribe's judgment about who I date about as well as I can trust mine," wrote Alex from Seattle. "They know me about as well as I know myself."

"I eventually decided that my friends' opinions usually proved more right about a guy than mine were," confirmed Katharine, thirty-two, from Boston. "If they didn't like him, I would usually get out of the relationship before I wasted too much time."

I noticed an interesting parallel here between how tribes judged new romantic partners and the role parents once had in this regard. Alex saw this too when he wrote: "Tribes are like having an Italian mother who wants to set you up, and if she isn't setting you up, she wants to know who you are with and what you are doing, and if she thinks the girl you're dating is a tramp, she's going to tell you."

"It's always challenging introducing a new or potential boyfriend to the crew," Christina, thirty-two, from Raleigh wrote. "If they don't fit in with the tribe, you pretty much have to jettison them. It's much worse than having them meet the parents."

Maybe no worse, however, than having a boyfriend or girlfriend meet your parents if you lived a hundred years ago. Those who believed courtship is dead in our times clearly don't understand the gauntlet to which friends subject new suitors. In modern courtship, it seems we no longer needed the approval of our distant parents – we need the approval of our tribes.

Unfortunately, I discovered reasons to believe that tribes might be less trustworthy in wielding this gatekeeping power than parents from previous generations would be. The question of motivations was critical. It was true that parents of old might have had different criteria than their sons and daughters as to what made a suitable mate. Parents might have preferred that their daughters date boring barbers to charismatic vaudevillians, but in all likelihood they wanted their children to ultimately enter happy marriages. In our time, it wasn't clear to me whether tribes could be counted on to share that goal.

Andrew Versus the Tribe: Round Two

Faced with her group's ultimatum, Jill chose Andrew over the tribe. The split did not happen all at once. Because Andrew was no longer welcome at most group events, Jill showed up less and less. She protested to her friends that Andrew made her happy, and it angered her that he was being boxed out of the group.

The tribe did not relent; in fact, as Jill drifted away, the sanctions grew more severe. Her individual friendships with group members became increasingly strained. Although they had enjoyed her company for years, members of the group now openly wondered about Jill's character. That she would be attracted to someone like Andrew and allow herself to be treated with such disrespect, they whispered to each other, meant that she was not the Jill they had thought they'd known.

The tribe's censure had the unintended consequence of making Jill invest more heavily in her relationship with Andrew. Within a year she had moved in with him. Members of the tribe heard rumors that they were talking about marriage.

It was not very long after Jill and Andrew had shacked up that it became clear that the tribe had been right about Andrew. A year and a half after they met, Andrew broke up with Jill suddenly. It came out that there had been a romance at work. Andrew was revealed to be an untrustworthy jerk, just as the group had surmised. Jill was heartbroken, and the tribe quickly rallied to support her. Friends let her sleep in their apartments while she got back on her feet. They loaned her money for a deposit on a new place. They threw her a big birthday party, and they made sure she had something to do or someone to be with nearly every night.

If there was one thing that tribes were good at, it was helping members through their breakups. I heard many stories from people like Betsy, thirty-two, from Palo Alto, who told me that after she was heartbroken, her tribe pooled money to fly her to New York, where they had rented a house at the beach for a long weekend. "They arranged everything and took care of it all, from airline reservation to cooking," she said. "I just packed a suitcase and showed up at the airport."

Katharine told me that her tribe makes up nicknames for suitors. "This makes it easier when they ditch you or you have to ditch them," she wrote. "For example, some exes of tribe members are known as 'Psycho Movie Bitch,' 'Bug Eyes,' 'Gay Virgin'; and one is identified by mimicking his annoying laugh."

I felt there was something suspicious about the often joyful energy tribes put into assisting heartbroken members. As with Betsy's free weekend on the beach or Jill's birthday party, there seemed a celebratory aspect to these efforts. It was often unclear to me whether tribes were helping the individual mourn a loss or rejoicing in his or her return to the fold.

It seemed to me that this conflict of interest was present in how tribes assessed mates as well. Just because Jill's tribe was ultimately right about Andrew did not mean that their motives were unselfish. If we look back at their actions, none of them took the time to understand the intimate connections between Jill and Andrew, nor did they look for any subtle or private strengths in their relationship. They judged Andrew mostly on his group behavior. Because he came from a different social world, Andrew was behind the eight ball from the beginning. Truth be told, many of the men didn't like him initially because they were jealous of his success. Given his reception, I was not surprised that his group behavior was always found wanting. Andrew most likely recognized that trying for acceptance in the group was a losing game. It was hard to blame him for not wanting to play.

Of course, tribes don't reject all new suitors. I heard many stories of new boyfriends and girlfriends fitting in. "The same week I met my boyfriend, Sam, there was a group trip to the mountain that weekend," wrote Mary from Pittsburgh. "I took Sam, figuring it was a trial by fire. If he couldn't get along with them – he was outta there. Fortunately, everyone liked him."

But even with such a happy outcome, I was not certain that Mary and her tribe had the same interest at heart. I came to believe that tribes accepted or rejected new suitors not because they individually liked or disliked them and not out of some judgment about whether they were the right fit for the tribe member in question. Rather, the tribe reaction to a new mate was based largely on the perception of whether the new boyfriend or girlfriend was going to steal away the established member. The problem was that any serious relationship – especially those headed for marriage – held the potential of pulling a member away from the tribe. We wanted the best for our tribemates, but at the same time we didn't want to be left behind.

Marriage and Children: Kryptonite to the Tribe?

People I interviewed and corresponded with had radically differing opinions about whether marriage and the tribe were compatible. From the perspective of being within the tribe, it was hard for people to imagine a future without their group. Marty hoped that her tribe members would eventually find mates but settle down near each other:

"I have a dream of living on the same cul de sac someday so that our children can all play together."

At the other extreme were those who had seen tribe members abandon the group upon getting married. When I asked Jeffrey, thirty-two, of Boston how marriage affects tribe membership, he wrote succinctly: "It kills. They leave." Brian, twenty-seven, from London, wrote just as tersely: "Marriage is the ticket out of the tribe." Or perhaps not all the way out and not all at once. "Those who've gotten married or pair up tend to drop into the background or stop visiting completely," wrote Mitch from Dallas.

This appeared particularly true if the bride or groom of the tribe member was never fully integrated into the tribe life before the marriage. "What I have seen happen is that the married ones are invited out less with the single members because sometimes, only one member of the couple was a member of the tribe and the new spouse never really fit in," wrote Monya, thirty-three, from Seattle. "I would say the most direct impact is that the newly married person stops spending the majority of their free time with the group."

"Only one guy has been married, and he dropped out of the group when that happened five years ago," Mark from Seattle wrote of his tribe of six male friends. "Recently marriage has been making a resurgence. A couple guys have gotten engaged, and I don't know how it will turn out. It's possible that the group will fragment. As a cohesive unit, I think our days may be numbered."

As if to resist this threat to the group, some tribes have tried to coopt the meaning of marriage rituals. When I talked to Cristi from New York, her group was in the middle of starting the ritual of having "single showers." "These would be like bridal showers but without the stupid groom," she explained. "I look at it this way. We haven't inconvenienced anyone with our weddings or anniversaries. So why shouldn't we get stuff too? We should be rewarded for staying single for this long."

Even mock weddings have become a microtrend among tribes composed of people in their early twenties. According to an article in the *New York Times*, "dozens of men and women in their late teens and early 20s have been putting on costly pseudo-weddings, complete with ceremony, reception and festivities." In one of these weddings two nonromantically involved friends in a Providence tribe were "married." The "bride" was carried to the altar on a rocking horse and the "groom" wore a bear suit.

These mock weddings seemed to hold a mixture of messages. On one level, they were signs that the next wave of young adults had fundamentally shifted their conception of when the right time for marriage was. They were having their mock weddings at exactly the same age that adults in the sixties were expected to get married for real. One mock bride, a college senior at the University of Wisconsin, told a reporter, "I know personally I won't be getting married for quite some time. There was so much detail that went into it, even for a mock wedding. I can't imagine planning a real wedding, now, at this age."

"It may be that marriage is so far off that people want to have the marriage experience now," said David Popenoe, a sociology professor at Rutgers University and an expert in the study of marriage trends. "Since they won't get married for a long time, they want the make-believe."

Mock weddings appeared also to be kind of a warning to others their age not to get married prematurely. Brooks, the bear-bridegroom at the Providence mock wedding, said the group wanted to have the ceremony because they liked attending weddings but didn't think anyone their age should be getting hitched. "It was really depressing to go to weddings that people our age were having," he said, adding that people who married in their young twenties were "ruining their lives." The fact that the "bride" was carried to the altar on a rocking horse was no doubt a symbol that she was too young for the real thing.

At their heart, I believed, these mock weddings were a way young tribes tried to inure themselves to the transformative power of marriage. They could see that marriage was the next major transition on the horizon – and by embracing it in a mock-serious way, they could sap the institution of some of its power.

But for tribes composed of people in their late twenties and thirties, marriage posed a much more ominous threat to the cohesiveness of the group. And the group, in turn, often posed an ominous hurdle to the individual's ability to make a graceful transition into marriage. We simply could not count on our friends to be selfless enough to let us move on in our lives, facing, as they were, the possibility that we might leave them behind.

"I've had the mentality that women come and go and that the tribe is forever," wrote David, twenty-seven, of San Francisco. "I have recently changed my mind and realized that friends are not forever – they ebb and flow and change over time. Expecting consistency is naïve. In retrospect, I might have been more dedicated to my tribe than was wise."

I assumed when I started looking into tribes that they came into existence to fill the vacuum created by the absence of young marriages and family. The truth was that tribal life was partly responsible for that very delay, or, more specifically, for why the delay lasted so long.

One Man's Story of Change

I was nearly ten years older than David was when I came to the same uncomfortable conclusion he had. I had been through three serious multiyear relationships and something approaching a dozen shorter fiascos. Every one of those relationships was in some ways damaged or held back by my life in the tribe. There were times when the group expressed its collective dislike for one or another of my girlfriends, but the most pervasive conflict came down to the basic question of where my loyalties lay. Even in the relationships where the girlfriend and the tribe got on famously, there was always the question of which I would pick if, someday, it came down to choosing one or the other.

Usually the conflict began in earnest when I would try to explain to a girlfriend that I wanted to attend a group event or take a group trip without her. This request often sparked an insidious type of jealousy – a suspicion on my girlfriend's part that I cared more for this strangely intimate group of friends than I did for her.

In other situations, a girlfriend would worry that if she did not measure up to my friends I would lose interest. Usually this meant that she would avoid going to group events in the hopes of luring me away from the social scene so that she didn't have to compete with it directly. It didn't help that these friends were everywhere in my life. I lived with some, I worked with others; I could bump into members of my tribe at almost any local event or happening. For the woman who wanted my exclusive attention, it must have seemed like she was battling a swarm of flies.

My girlfriends were right to be jealous. Whenever it came time to calculate a relationship's potential for going the distance, I elected to continue my tribe years. I regret none of those decisions. None of those women were right for me. It sometimes angered me when my tribe made that assessment before I did, but in the end they were always right. In fact, without their input and social support, I might very well have fallen into a doomed early marriage.

I was halfway through my thirty-seventh year when things changed for me. I met a beautiful and charming woman at a multi-tribe Halloween party. (To answer the inevitable next question: She was dressed as Betty Rubble and I was a fireman's Dalmatian.) The fact that Rebecca was there at all was testimony to the weak ties that connected my tribe to San Francisco. She was relatively new to the city and was there through a friend of a friend. My tribe should get credit in another way. Having the rest of my group at the party also gave me the confidence to ask Rebecca to dance.

The next week, after having dinner on our first date, I invited her to come with me to a friend's house where my tribe had gathered to watch the presidential election results. Having yet to fully understand the tribe-versus-love dynamics detailed above, I figured it was never too early to see how she got along with everybody. Despite the history of the tribe eclipsing my romantic life, I naïvely thought of my membership in the group as one of my selling points. Wouldn't I look more attractive when she saw what interesting and accomplished friends I had?

Fortunately, she declined that invitation. She was a psychiatric resident and had been up for much of the previous thirty-six hours. It was her ridiculous schedule that helped us get off on the right foot. She had so little time for me that in the few evenings she was free, I wanted her attention all to myself. In this way, I began an romantic life that was not connected to or under the scrutiny of my tribe.

As Rebecca allowed me more into her life, the momentum of my life shifted from the tribe to this new relationship. I stopped regularly attending our group's Tuesday-night dinners. I heard grumbling from my friends. Although my house was Tribe Central, I stopped throwing barbecues or holding game nights on a regular basis. I was no longer interested in carousing around town with the single guys in the group.

Some friends expressed in no uncertain terms that they felt hurt and said that I was turning my back on them. I would tell them that they were overreacting. I still showed up at many group functions. I was still their friend. But they were right that change was in the air. If things worked out with Rebecca, I would have to ask all my many roommates to find new homes.

I was in the process of changing my definition of "us" from meaning "the group" to meaning "Rebecca and me." It became clear to me that I could not ask my friends' permission to make this transition. It was a risk I had to take on my own. As frightening as it was, I had to take a break from my central role in the tribe if I was going to give my relationship with Rebecca a chance. Love is a leap of faith that you cannot fully commit to if you can see your friends busily building a safety net below.

Taking a break from my group was necessary for another reason. My friends had seen me screw up my romantic life for fifteen years running. I had the well-deserved reputation in their eyes as a fuck-up boyfriend – always conflicted and confused in my relationships with women. Often I didn't really mind this reputation. It was the source of endless playful teasing. But once I was in a relationship that I hoped might be The One, that reputation haunted me. I needed to convince Rebecca – and, as important, myself – that I could do better, that it was not my fate to screw up. To do that required the illusion of a clean slate, which was impossible to maintain if my friends were there to subtly or not so subtly remind me of my past failures. I needed to distance myself from the tribe for the same reason that we take leave of our parents to become adults. To grow up, you have to move away from the people who remember how you cried in the dark and wet your bed.

I was in the process of forming the idea for this book when Rebecca and I began to talk about our long-term future together. She had had her own tribe when she was in medical school in L.A. and immediately understood what I was talking about. Beginning my exit from the tribe years at the same time that I worked to try and document their meaning proved remarkably helpful. I had an open forum to express how grateful I was for having this time of life, even as it began to end.

I don't mean to set up such a black-and-white conflict between love and the tribe. When Rebecca and I announced that we were engaged to be married, my friends – each and every one of them – expressed their happiness for us. They all promised to dance at our wedding. More than dance, actually: Larry and Richard promised to play music, Rea promised to be the mistress of ceremonies, Jennifer and Allison promised to decorate, Po consented to officiate.

My tribal life and the friendships that comprised it did not end the moment I got engaged, but they certainly continued to change. What would eventually happen to my relationship to this group? I did not know the answer to that question, but it was something I was looking forward to figuring out. I knew one thing for sure: I had this group of people to thank for seeing me safely to this point. Actually, I had them to thank for much more than that. The devotion my friends showed me over the years taught me what devotion meant. That was knowledge I would rely on when I became a husband and someday, maybe, a father. I could also say this with confidence: I would not have grown into the man that Rebecca wanted to marry without them.

Epilogue

ONE MAN'S TRANSITION

I write from Hawaii. I'm in a hotel room near the beach and I'm smack-dab in the middle of my weeklong honeymoon. With this book's deadline fast approaching, my new wife (wife, wife, wife, wife – it will be a while before I get used to that word) has encouraged me take some time and finish it up. I have the sliding glass door open; the air is thick and smells of tropical flowers that I imagine to be huge and white. Although I'm forgoing a morning at the beach, I'm glad to have the chance to write from this present-tense perspective, perched as I am at the end of my single years, suddenly part of a traditional family again.

I realized an interesting fact recently while thinking about the time I've spent living outside a family: My wedding day was exactly twenty years from the day my mother and father drove me out of town to drop me off at the dorm rooms of my university. I have spent exactly twenty years – almost to the hour – living outside a family unit. It's hard not to look for a message in such a fact. One thing is clear: it is impossible to see such a large chunk of time (what will likely turn out to be more than a quarter of my life) as a transitional phase between youth and adulthood. Twenty years is an era – a goddamned *epoch* of one's existence.

There are very few things I wish I could change about those two decades, but there are many things I wish I had known. I wish I had known, for instance, that such a long period of being single was in the cards for me. I also wish I'd known earlier that such a delay was not abnormal among my generation. As it was, I spent the first ten years of living outside a family feeling like a traveler stuck in between places. If I had known I'd be there for so long, I think I would have spent less time gazing down the road, looking for the next bus out of town. I certainly would have taken the time to paint some of my apartments and bought nicer furniture.

It seems like it was only in the second decade of living single that I settled into that life. It took me that long to understand that that style of life was nothing to be ashamed or afraid of, and that the tribe years had rhythms and reasons of their own. I was long into my second decade of living single before I came to see my friends in the city for what they were: my personal community, my urban tribe.

Here's another thing I wish I had known: I wish someone could have told me that it was all going to turn out so well. If I'd known that someday I would be on such a happy honeymoon, I could have given up the constant worry that there was something deeply wrong with me that was keeping me from falling in love and getting married. After so many years of being single and so many failed romances of varying severities, that worry showed up every night, ringing my doorbell just as I was trying to fall off to sleep.

Of course, knowing that things will work out well is not possible. One of the paradoxes of the tribe years is that the happier and more content one is being single, the more one suspects that a happy marriage might not be in the cards. It's easy to mistakenly assume that being good at being single means that one is bad at getting married. It is also true that being single feels like an open-ended state until the day things change. One day you're in a funk about things, telling a friend that years of evidence point to the conclusion that you will be single for the rest of your life. That night you meet someone, and a year later you're engaged to be married. That this very scenario happened to me is likely of little comfort to those still wondering about their future. However, my sincere hope that things work out for all the yet-to-be-marrieds is no bland anodyne. Sociologists who seem to know about these things say that the vast majority of us will still get hitched.

Of course, marriage will elude some, and others will opt to avoid it. Our record-setting delay will no doubt be followed by a record number of people who never marry. Those people will continue our generation's unique challenge of making up a life story outside the narratives provided by traditional family life. Remaining single through one's forties, fifties, and sixties will no doubt have its unique challenges and rewards. While these forever-singles will likely be a small percentage of my generation, I imagine there will be enough of them to create an influential cultural force. They will not, it's safe to say, meekly play out their days living in rented rooms. Whether they will continue to live through urban tribes or find ways to integrate into families, I do not know. Given how well the last twenty years have gone for me, however, I have faith that these forever-singles will find happiness and satisfaction in their lives. I am looking forward to hearing the story of that demographic group as it unfolds.

The delay will also, inevitably, mean that a substantial number of couples from my generation will not have children. Some will choose not to have children and some will be unable to conceive. It is possible that Rebecca and I will fall into this latter category. To have deeply desired children and have missed that opportunity because you happened to be caught in the shifting social trends of your time may be a tragedy for some. However, I doubt there will be a large number of people who go through their middle years mourning the children they never had. The human creature is more resilient, forward-looking, and innately hopeful than that. Faced with a reality such as staying single for life or getting married too late to have children, women and men will simply shift and find new goals for their lives. Some will even misremember their younger ambivalence, convincing themselves that they never wanted to have children in the first place. This is the power of the mind to morph our desires to fit the reality of our circumstances. If I've learned anything from the last twenty years, it is that our hopes and plans shape our lives far less than our lives shape our hopes and plans.

The Fog of Memory

Twenty years. I can already sense memory doing its work – caramelizing those times into the stuff of nostalgia. Many memories from those twenty years have become unstuck in time. I can't remember whom I was going out with the year my group took that trip to the Utah salt flats or whether the year of the Loma Prieta earthquake was the same year I moved from Bush Street to the Haight-Ashbury District. It is all something of a blur. How can I even begin to convey those twenty years of memories?

Maybe by sharing just one. Since I'm at the very end of one stage of my life, let me go all the way back to its beginning – nearly twenty years ago. I remember a particular summer's day after I had completed my first year at college. My childhood friend Sean and I were driving in his white Toyota Corolla out of our small Central Valley college town on our way to San Francisco. We had worked for the first part of the summer and had a little money and a month to blow before we had to be back at school. For the first time in our lives, all the decisions were ours to make. A mutual friend had ended up in San Francisco, and we were going to stay with her for a while. It was a Friday, and there was a party in Berkeley that she had told us she could probably get us into. That seemed promising. It all seemed promising. The month we had to ourselves felt like an endless expanse of time.

Sean and I had both grown up in the same small town, and San Francisco frightened us a bit, although we wouldn't have admitted this to each other. It was the sort of fright that you get on a roller-coaster ride, the kind of nervousness and thrill of the unexpected that you learn to love and crave. The potential for what might happen in the city was intoxicating. Sean drove fast with the windows down, and we had to yell at each other to be heard above the wind.

To drive out of the Central Valley of California on a hot day and into San Francisco is to feel like you're landing on another planet. Over our two-hour drive, the temperature went from nearly a hundred to the middle sixties. The visual disparity was as dramatic. On one side of the bay was a day so bright you'd have to squint with the visor down and your sunglasses on. Halfway across the Bay Bridge the fog enveloped us, whipping in strands through the rusted girders. As we crossed into the fog, it didn't seem possible that two such environments could exist side by side. The wind buffeted the car so hard that Sean drove with his hands locked to wheel.

Coming off the Bay Bridge in the middle lane, Sean was too nervous of city traffic to merge aggressively, and we missed our exit. We tried to double back but instantly got lost. This is how young we were: The idea of buying a map didn't occur to us. Instead, we crisscrossed the town looking for the street names that we would recognize from Peggy's directions. We were both in shorts, and neither of us had thought to bring a jacket. We rolled up the windows and turned on the heat. The city swallowed us.

We were too excited to be scared. Besides, we already could see how we would manage it all. Eventually we would call Peggy and she would tell us where to go. If we didn't get into the party that night, there would be another tomorrow. We were both good at making friends. We would endear ourselves to people. We'd find a social toehold and begin to learn from new acquaintances how people created their lives here – lives that might have little to do with parents or teachers or what you said you were going to be when you were growing up in a small town.

It has been a long time since I've gotten lost in San Francisco. I've learned what I've needed to know about living in the city. I know what goes on at night and I know what is likely to be happening around the next corner. The raving lunatics who wander around City Hall no longer fascinate me. I am neither shocked nor particularly amused when a herd of bearded men wearing nothing but chaps cross the road in front of my car. Some of the city's mysteries and carnival charms have vanished. Yet, as I remember that first day when I entered the city on my own terms, I know that a kernel of that feeling stayed with me all through the next two decades. I never completely lost that sense of giddy freedom we felt.

Did I stay too long at the fair? I don't think so (but I'm willing to concede that an objective third party might conclude that I did). Looking from this vantage point, it seems like that part of my life took the amount of time that it needed to take. Sometimes it takes a long time to put your talents, weaknesses, and proclivities into the mix of a city and see what's going to happen.

Freedom and Its Discontents

Sentimentality is the sin of the memoirist. I'm being too sentimental, I know. To be perfectly honest, I don't even exactly know how much of that memory from nineteen years ago is true. Was that our first college summer vacation or the next year? Was it really that cold that day? Am I mixing in a memory from six years ago, when Sean and I drove back to San Francisco after a fishing trip, with him on his way home to his wife and child? Before I let it go, before I let memory mix it all up and smooth its edges (simultaneously letting it fade from view), I will try to remember it without nostalgia. It already takes an effort, a certain mental discipline, to remember any of the disappointments and nagging dissatisfactions of those years.

That I could mix up something that happened nineteen years ago with something that happened six years ago is emblematic of one of the frustrations of that time. It is hard to distinguish between those memories because the person I was at twenty and the person I was at thirty-one seemed nearly identical. Every year the feeling that nothing ever changed became increasingly disturbing.

Sometimes I lost sense of time completely. When I was visiting home one year, my father asked me when I was planning on buying a house of my own. I said maybe in fifteen years or so. "In fifteen years you'll be fifty," he said to me. It's embarrassing to tell you all the reasons this shocked me. The math he had done was so simple (although I was only thirty-four at the time), but my mind didn't seem willing to believe it. The moment also revealed just how confused I was over the very nature of time as it applied to the passage of my life. Truth was, I had not had any sort of plan to buy a house in fifteen years. I had just picked the number out of the air, not having any sense of the value of fifteen years or the idea that one might endeavor to chart a life into that far a future. It seemed weirdly possible that fifteen years could go by and I might be the very same person. After all, it felt like nothing much had changed in the previous fifteen years.

Of course it wasn't true that nothing had changed. Significant things were constantly changing in my life – big things like girlfriends, apartments, and jobs. Only two years after that conversation with my father, I even managed to buy the house my roommates and I had been renting for the previous five years. The problem was that these changes didn't feel anything like a progression. Although these modifications were usually clear improvements, they seemed haphazard, picaresque turns of good fortune. I think the human mind desires not only that change be positive but that it happen as part of a sequence that gives us sense of forward momentum. Despite all the good things that have happened to me in the last twenty years, that sense of progression is one thing that my life has decidedly lacked.

With each year, even as I became more comfortable with my social life in the tribe, I developed a greater thirst for that elusive forward momentum – a desire not just for change but for a next stage, marriage, which would lead to the next stage, children. To delay marriage so long is to dam up certain desires, hopes, and plans. With each passing year, the pressure builds a little. Then, with a little luck, you meet someone, and the floodgates open. After that, your life can feel like a torrent of change for a while. But to be moving forward again, even in such a wild current – what elation.

This joy came not simply from the sense of progress but from the feeling that a particular nagging burden had been lifted – specifically, the burden of having to create the story of my life on the fly. Marriage, of course, does not have to be lived in lockstep with other marriages, but there is an overall narrative structure to the thing. The story of a marriage begins with an engagement, then a wedding, then a honeymoon, and then the life choices begin – where to live, how to manage resources, whether or when to have children. No two marriages are the same, but because they have similar milestones, they can be compared with one another. Rebecca and I can, for instance, begin to compare our wedding ceremony with that of cousins who are planning theirs. We can compare the strengths and weaknesses of our union with those of our parents and brothers and sisters.

Our embrace of that narrative structure is perhaps best expressed by our choice of Hawaii as our honeymoon destination. Outside of Niagara Falls, it's hard to imagine a less adventurous or more prepackaged honeymoon. Of course we knew how clichéd this was, but that was its attraction. We wanted to go to a place where every bellhop and waiter assumed we were newlyweds. We wanted the constant reminders that we were beginning the story of being married.

There were more than two dozen other newlyweds on our flight to Kauai. They were easily identified by their lovey-dovey affect, the man's penchant for fussing with his new ring, and the woman's unchipped French-manicured nails. Besides those similarities, none of us looked the same. There was everything from buzz-cut, tow-headed grooms with their blond brides from the Midwest to a tattooed hipster couple from Brooklyn. (Even the tattooed-hipster bride had the French manicure. Some mother, or mother-in-law, had put her foot down.) There was also a dramatic range of ages. Next to us at the airport bar was a couple whose combined age was distressingly near my own. But despite our differences we smiled and toasted each other with coffee cups and Bloody Marys. We were pleased to be in each other's company. Having all gotten married on the same fall day, the beginning of the story of our married lives all shared the same detail.

I suspect that I am again a bellwether. My desire to share in the traditional narrative of marriage and family seems to mirror a general cultural shift. I believe the next ten years will not see the marriage delay continue to grow at the pace it has over the last decade. The pendulum may even swing back some. A season ago, only three family shows ranked in the top thirty among the coveted eighteen-to-forty-eight-year-old market. This season, fully *nine* family shows made that list. Even NBC, which rode the tribe phenomenon with *Friends, Seinfeld*, and *Will and Grace*, seemed to be shifting its focus both by marrying two of the *Friends* characters and investing in two new family comedies.

I don't expect my marriage to Rebecca to resemble those of the couples on those television shows or the newlyweds with whom we shared the flight last Sunday. I don't expect our marriage to be like the marriages of our parents. To share a story structure is not to share the same story. I have reason to expect that it will be every bit the adventure the last twenty years provided. I'm sure, in its own way, our marriage will push the boundaries of the narrative. I am from a generation that, in delaying marriage so long, chose an unexpected path. I don't think that propensity for choosing new paths will end with our weddings.

Admitting to the Bias That Makes This Entire Book Suspect

I know that when one is given endless amounts of evidence from which to form a theory, one inevitably "finds" in that evidence proof for the assumptions that one started out looking for. I am no exception to this proclivity. Having spent many years living single, I have an unavoidable bias to "discover" that those years were not wasted, that they were, in fact, filled to the brim with meaning and importance. I want to believe that my friends and I strove to do worthy things during those years – find true love, create art, or search for spiritual peace. I want to believe that even as we sometimes tilted at windmills, we managed to establish friendships and groups of friends that supported us in topsy-turvy times. I found evidence for all these things, but I also know that I started out hoping to find just such good news.

Did my hoping to find these things in my generation make them appear? Was I just reaching into such a large hat of evidence that I could pull out whatever rodent I chose? Almost certainly. No doubt, had I been hell-bent on creating the opposite argument (that the marriage delay was the epitome of immaturity and self-centeredness), I could easily have marshaled anecdotal evidence to buttress that case as well.

But even as I know that I doggedly looked for good news, I can't leave behind the idea that my conclusions are true. Such is the certainty of the mind that sits before a book of hand-chosen evidence. I both believe it to be true and know I wanted it to be true at the same time. I feel no shame in the wanting part. I know that in delving into the lives of the yet-to-be-marrieds, I've become an unabashed promoter of the potential of those years. In describing urban tribes, I hope to push people toward them and remind people to look for meaning in them sooner than later.

What will happen next? In the last year, I've focused on only two things. I've built a relationship with Rebecca, and I've written this book. My life in the tribe became, for the first time in my adult life, a distant third. But at our wedding last Saturday, they were all there standing shoulder to shoulder in our backyard. And it is from the spirit of that wedding that I hope to create the next stage of my life. The "us" in my world has shrunk to mean Rebecca and me, but we intend to find a way to use the energy that still exists from my tribe years.

Rebecca and I are one of the first couples out of our group to get married. Already there is another engagement, however, and rumors of another. I suspect there will be more betrothals within the year. I imagine there will be years when we all focus on our young marriages and then children. But when those children get old enough to begin forming their own social circles, we'll gravitate together again. Someone will have a summer house where we'll gather. I could go on about this fantasy future, but why imagine future joy when your life is full of happiness in the present? Right now the sun is shining, I can hear the ocean crashing about, and my new wife awaits.

ACKNOWLEDGMENTS

Of course it's redundant to say that I have my tribe of friends to thank. All of them gave me some type of help or emotional support during this process. Larry Gallagher, in particular, helped me out. He has always been a supportive friend, even when he disagrees with me. This book could not have been completed without another good friend, Sean Wagstaff, who set up my Web site www.urbantribes.net, through which I gathered so much information about tribes around the world. Larry and Sean's no-questions-asked willingness to shoulder part of my burden is the spirit of the urban tribe.

Paul Tough; Rob Riddel; Matthew Igoe; my mother, Mary Watters; my brother, Aaron Watters, and sister in-law, Nancy Laparo; all helped out at different times, either with conceptual or with specific advice. Po Bronson, who kindly blurbed this book, also gave me sage advice all the way through its creation. Mandy Erickson was an excellent copy editor on the first draft. The two dozen writers at the San Francisco Writers' Grotto (Noah Hawley and Mary Roach in particular) deserve thanks for their support of this project. Rebecca, to whom this book is dedicated, encouraged me every day and even tried to laugh at the parts in chapter 6 where I portrayed myself as a numbskull.

Over a thousand people from around the country took time to give me their thoughts and share stories from their lives. This book is my humble thank-you for that outpouring of help.

The entire staff at Bloomsbury has been fantastic. My editor, Colin Dickerman, and agent, Jay Mandel, made me feel as smart as they are and were generous in their support from the first word to the last.

A NOTE ON THE AUTHOR

Ethan Watters lives and writes in San Francisco. He is happy but not necessarily because of the following details. Ethan has written extensively in the areas of psychology, group behavior, and coercion. His work has appeared in the *New York Times Magazine*, *Spin*, *Details*, *Mother Jones*, *GQ*, and *Esquire*, among other publications. He is a founder (along with Po Bronson and Ethan Canin) of the San Francisco Writers' Grotto, a collective workspace that currently houses twenty-one journalists, filmmakers, and novelists.

A NOTE ON THE TYPE

The text of this book is set in Linotype Sabon, named after the type founder, Jacques Sabon. It was designed by Jan Tschichold and jointly developed by Linotype, Monotype, and Stempel, in response to a need for a typeface to be available in identical form for mechanical hot metal composition and hand composition using foundry type.

Tschichold based his design for Sabon roman on a font engraved by Garamond, and Sabon italic on a font by Granjon. It was first used in 1966 and has proved an enduring modern classic.